VISION 2000
PLANNING FOR MINISTRY INTO THE NEXT CENTURY

JOE A. HARDING

RALPH W. MOHNEY

DISCIPLESHIP RESOURCES

MATERIALS FOR GROWTH IN CHRISTIAN FAITH & LIFE

— NASHVILLE, TENNESSEE —

D1066666

Reprinted 1994.

90,000 copies in print.

Fourth printing.

ISBN 0-88177-098-1

Library of Congress Catalog Card No. 90-62153

Unless otherwise indicated, all scripture quotations are taken from
the New Revised Standard Version of the Holy Bible, Copyright ©
1989 by The Division of Christian Education of the National Council
of the Churches of Christ in the U.S.A. and used by permission.

VISION 2000: Planning for Ministry into the Next Century. Copyright
© 1991 by Discipleship Resources. All rights reserved. Printed in the
United States of America. No part of this book may be reproduced in
any manner whatsoever without written permission except in the case
of brief quotations embodied in critical articles or reviews. For
information address Discipleship Resources Editorial Office, P.O. Box
840, Nashville, TN 37202.

DR098

CONTENTS

ACKNOWLEDGMENTS

We are grateful to many, many people who have contributed encouragement and inspiration to Vision 2000. We are grateful for congregations in Richland, Washington; Chattanooga, Tennessee; Kingsport, Tennessee; and Salem, Oregon. We have been greatly encouraged by the strong and consistent support of Vision 2000 by Ezra Earl Jones, General Secretary of the General Board of Discipleship and by the Evangelism staff.

The enthusiasm of Bishop Bevel Jones of the Western North Carolina Conference and Donald Haynes, his Director of Ministries, in adopting Vision 2000 as a major emphasis for their annual conference has been a tremendous inspiration to us. This program, developed by Don Haynes, hopefully is being shared across the church for use in districts and annual conferences.

We are grateful for the helpful suggestions that have come from Nell Mohney, our editor Craig Gallaway, and members of the Section on Evangelism of the General Board of Discipleship. A special word of thanks to Nadina Wooding, who spent hours and hours typing. She has been a strong and steady encouragement to meet the deadlines and to get the manuscript completed on time. To all of these wonderful people we say, "God bless you!" and a heartfelt "Thank you!"

PREFACE

"*The time is fulfilled, and the kingdom of God has come near; repent, and believe in the good news*" (Mark 1:15).

"*Hope alone is to be called 'realistic,' because it alone takes seriously the possibilities with which all reality is fraught*" (Jürgen Moltmann in *The Theology of Hope*).

"*I consider that the sufferings of this present time are not worth comparing with the glory about to be revealed to us. For the creation waits with eager longing for the revealing of the children of God*" (Romans 8:18-19).

"*We know that the whole creation has been groaning in labor pains until now*" (Romans 8:22).

"*. . . one thing I do: forgetting what lies behind and straining forward to what lies ahead, I press on toward the goal for the prize of the heavenly call of God in Christ Jesus*" (Philippians 3:13-14).

"*May the God of hope fill you with all joy and peace in believing, so that you may abound in hope by the power of the Holy Spirit*" (Romans 15:13).

INTRODUCTION: 2000
A MAGNETIC YEAR

A. "THE YEAR 2000 IS OPERATING LIKE A POWERFUL MAGNET on humanity, already reaching down into the 1990s and intensifying the decade. It is amplifying emotions, accelerating change, and heightening awareness, compelling us to re-examine ourselves, our values, and our institutions. . . . The year 2000 is not just a new century, but a religious experience related to the religious-revival megatrend."[1]

These words, by John Naisbitt and Patricia Aburdane in their best-seller *Megatrends 2000*, confront thoughtful Christians, lay and clergy, with the awareness that we are now facing what may well be "an unprecedented opportunity"! Many can see signs that unmistakably indicate the possibility of a worldwide religious revival as this third millennium begins. What direction will it take?

One thousand years ago, as Europe prepared for the coming of the second millennium, it was seized by what Bill Lawren, writing in *Psychology Today*, called "a paroxysm of preapocalyptic shivers."[2] Legend tells how on the stroke of midnight before January 1, 1000, the "population of an entire country, Iceland, converted *en masse* to Christianity, apparently as a spiritual prophylactic against the coming apocalypse."

Today evidence is mounting that this period will be used by some "end of the world" scenarists as their opportunity to spread the doctrines portrayed by many "doomsday" preachers and believers. If, however, this is all that happens as a new millennium is born, our planet will be much the poorer!

B. "VISION 2000" IS PRESENTED AS A POWERFUL CALL to all mainline Protestant congregations to prayerfully and expectantly re-visualize their future, so that by the year A.D. 2000 those congregations will be vital, caring, sharing, redemptive fellowships in ministry for Jesus Christ.

For too long too many congregations have suffered from a myopic image of death and decline, which has destroyed their vision, emasculated their power, and thwarted the efforts of deeply dedicated believers who have tried to rise above this paralyzing concept. Vision

2000 comes to affirm the words of Jesus when he said, "The time is fulfilled (now). The kingdom of God is at hand (now). The fields are already white for harvest (now)."

The year 2000 is a year in *chronos* time, yet it has unlimited *kairos* possibilities. These are the key words for time in the New Testament. *Chronos* deals with measurable calendar time, such as, "In the year that King Uzziah died" or "When Quinirius was governor of Syria. . . ." So, the year 2000 is a particular moment in measurable calendar time. The other word for time is *kairos*. *Kairos* is calendar time filled full of the activity of God. It is the word for time used in the opening verses of the Gospel of Mark: "The time *(kairos)* is fulfilled;. . . repent, and believe in the good news" (Mark 1:15). We contend that the calendar year 2000 has powerful *kairos* possibilities.

In these final years of the twentieth century, the church needs to embrace and to proclaim a balanced biblical view of the future. Some may come saying that religion is dead and that the church can't change or grow. Listen for the tone of their cynicism in a one-sidedly pessimistic notion of *chronos* time: "Time marches on. The future is already determined by the past. The year 2000 will be nothing more than another moment in the ongoing flow of historical days, weeks, and years. Time is fate." Looking at the future through this lens, who could possibly be inspired to seek fresh vision for the coming millennium?

On the other hand, there will be the "new-agers" and/or the apocalypticists. Both inside and outside the church, some will seem to be impressed only by promises of spectacular *kairos* time—some great moment or impending event that will allegedly alter and align our entire lives. We can be sure that the year 2000 will not escape such attention. Watch for the signs of such false romanticism in an impatience with the practical realities of sound management and long-range planning. For some, the idea of a vision for the next century will conjure nothing more than a desire to be on the right "mountain" at the right moment.

We believe that a truly biblical view of the future moves us beyond either of these counterfeits. Looking for God's future in the coming millennium, in biblical terms, will free us to embrace both *chronos* and *kairos*—both the historical day-to-day grind of "real" life, and the confidence that God can and does act in our history and in our time, "creating a new thing."

We hope to inspire you with the biblical accounts of how Moses, Abraham, Sarah, Isaiah, Ezekiel, Joshua, and others "leaned forward" into their future with hope and anticipation. We want you to see Jesus "leaning forward" into his commitment as he set his face "steadfastly" to go to Jerusalem. Then we want you to thrill to the meaning of that vision for you and your church. We want you to understand the motivating power of the early Christians as they "leaned forward" and moved from Jerusalem out to the uttermost parts of the world.

C. "VISION 2000 CONGREGATIONS AFFIRM THE POSTURE and the potential of bold faith, enthusiastic expectation, vital prayer, and committed obedience. They affirm that "with God's help, we will turn from our excuses, our evasions, and our apathy to a new sterling quality of commitment. We can and will see our future in a new way. We can and will know the transforming power and presence of Jesus Christ in our midst. We can and will be faithful in reaching out to individuals in the spirit of Christ, in sensitively helping them relate to him, in expectantly seeing the difference he makes in their lives, our lives, the life of the church, and the life of the world.

Yes, Vision 2000 congregations are hopeful! They are exciting, caring, and positive. They are creative, imaginative, courageous—always willing not only to be open to God's dreams and visions, but also to be a "co-laborer with Christ" in the work of his kingdom. They not only believe, but are willing to venture out on the conviction that God's dreams and visions are called into being through ordinary people— pastors and laity—and through ordinary congregations like yours.

You have now read far enough to know what is "envisioned" as a part of Vision 2000. The next question is, "Are you with us?" Are you willing to think of your congregation as one of a great flotilla of ships that is charting its course, choosing its direction, and steaming toward all that God has purposed for you to do and to become? Or is this too great an effort? Is it easier instead to disappear into the depths as some congregations seem committed to do?

Make no mistake about it. You and your congregation will experience the year 2000. How will you prepare for its coming? What difference will you make during these intervening years? Consider the fact that there are more people "out there" in our communities who are unrelated to the church and yet who need what the church has to offer, than ever before. They and others, if properly approached, are more than willing to "taste and see" if your church, your faith, your love, and your discipleship are for them.

Will you become a "Vision 2000 Church"?

1 | STEPS TO TAKE AT THIS TIME

This is the first of several pages entitled "Steps to Take at This Time." You will also find additional "Steps to Take" at the close of Chapters 4, 6, and 7. These can be read in advance to give you a working knowledge of the procedure that will be followed. We wish to capitalize on the inspiration and information being presented in the text of this study. Procedural instructions are of the greatest importance if you and your congregation are to successfully fulfill all of the possibilities wrapped up in this dynamic approach to ministry in the next century.

AFTER READING THE INTRODUCTION

1. The pastor should carefully choose two key leaders and ask them to read through the entire book.

2. After reading the text, the pastor and two leaders should meet and evaluate this resource, answering these questions honestly:

   a. Does this opportunity for study, reflection, and action have merit for us? Why?

   b. Does the Vision 2000 concept inspire us? Motivate us? Make us eager to discover what God can do here?

   c. Can we interpret this challenge to some of the ablest people in our membership and form a Vision 2000 Team?

   d. Will this team be prepared to work through the study guide process that is integral to this workbook? (Each of the first eight chapters includes questions for indepth reflection, discussion, and review. Team members must be prepared to share in this process wholeheartedly.)

   e. How many should we invite to be part of the team? (We suggest from six to twelve; larger congregations ten to twenty.)

   f. Who should be included? Are they positive, eager, representative of the age groups, and able to give the time?

3. If these questions are answered in a way that indicates interest, then a second set of questions must be answered:

   a. Has the governing body of our congregation been *informed* of the plan to create a Vision 2000 Team? (In order to "free" the team for its own role, and though there may be some overlap, it will usually work best if the Vision 2000 Team is not identical to the governing body of the congregation. The role of the governing body is to "authorize" and to encourage vision, not to "gate-keep" it.)

b. Does the governing body *understand* the basic structure of the Vision 2000 plan—including the procedures in Chapters 1 through 8 for creating a vision and reporting it to the congregation? (The pastor and two key leaders could accomplish this as a special presentation to the governing body.)

c. Has the governing body *affirmed* the plan for a Vision 2000 Team, and is this body prepared to *recognize* and to *support* the work of the Team as the *vision* unfolds? (One very effective way of launching the entire program would be to have a special "Commissioning Service" during which, in front of the whole congregation, the governing body commissions the Vision 2000 Team to its task and pledges to support the team with bold faith into the future.)

4. When the governing body has approved the Vision 2000 concept, you are ready for a final set of first steps:

a. Begin the selection of the Vision 2000 Team.

b. Schedule all the meetings in advance so members can know what they will be involved in and when. It is anticipated that eleven sessions will be needed to complete the full study and the actions that follow.

c. Each chapter of the text will require one session. Where needed, however, such as in Chapter 7, two sessions will be required to complete that study.

d. Plan to begin meeting as soon as Team members have a copy and have read the manual, *Vision 2000*.

5. Plan to make the first session a memorable experience.

a. Plan for it carefully.

b. Open with the words of Isaiah: "I am about to do a new thing; now it springs forth, do you not perceive it?" (Isaiah 43:19). Affirm to each other your belief that God is now doing and will do new things for you and your congregation.

c. Each Team member should read the chapter and complete the questions for that chapter before attending the next session. Answers should be written in the manual for future reference.

d. Select your Vision 2000 Team and begin your study!

I | EXPLORING THE "WHY" OF VISION 2000

"Comparatively few pastors have developed a vision for ministry. Not surprisingly, it is the rare lay person who has emerged from the pack with an articulate, coherent, long-range vision for either the local church or a personal ministry."[3] Such an indictment prompts us to deal with this tragic deficiency.

Leaders at almost every level of the church tend to think in very short time blocks. For many mainline Protestant congregations, four years is considered long-term planning. With the frequent pastoral changes, the larger vision is forgotten in favor of maintenance issues. This leads to the development of thousands of passive, reactive churches.

Vision-receptive congregations are challenged in this manual to think in terms of ten-year goals! Such long-term visions can be "owned" by the congregation. The church thus becomes leadership change-proof! Clergy and lay leadership may change. The vision remains and inspires.

Positive anticipation of the future, inspired by great dreams and visions, unites and energizes the congregation! Visions have a unifying, forward pull. Lack of vision leads to confusion, absence of purpose, and a growth of meaningless busyness. Vision is essential for the ministry of the church in a new century.

Many people customarily label any visionary approach to ministry as naive, romantic, and unrealistic. Yet, faithful visionary thinking is to be called realistic. It takes seriously the power of God, working through people, to create a new future.

You already recognize the importance of vision. Perhaps you are now thinking of the passage from the Book of Proverbs, "Where there is no vision, the people perish" (Proverbs 29:18, KJV). For several good reasons we can have confidence in the power of vision:

A. GOD IS A VISION-SHARING GOD. It is the nature of God to share vision with people who need direction.

The people of Israel had suffered devastating defeat. Jerusalem lay in ruins. The walls had been battered to mere rubble. People had been transported as exiles into Babylon. Hopelessness and despair were everywhere. In that devastating situation, God gave the prophet Ezekiel a great vision (Ezekiel 37:1-14).

Ezekiel saw a great valley in which many bones were dried up and bleached. The bones were a tragic reminder of the defeat of the people at the hands of a ruthless enemy. In the vision, Ezekiel heard God ask, "Mortal, can these bones live?" Of course Ezekiel did not know. He answered, "O Lord God, you know."

God said: "Prophesy to these bones, and say to them: O dry bones, hear the word of the Lord. Thus says the Lord God to these bones: I will cause breath to enter you, and you shall live. I will lay sinews on you, and will cause flesh to come upon you, and cover you with skin, and put breath in you, and you shall live; and you shall know that I am the Lord."

Ezekiel saw himself preaching to that unlikely congregation. The response was amazing: ". . . Suddenly there was a noise, a rattling, and the bones came together, bone to its bone." Then Ezekiel saw sinews, flesh, and skin upon the bones. Still, there was no life, only dead bodies. And God said, "Prophesy to the breath, prophesy, mortal, and say to the breath: Thus says the Lord God: Come from the four winds, O breath, and breathe upon these slain, that they may live." So Ezekiel prophesied as God commanded, and "breath came into them, and they lived, and stood on their feet, a vast multitude."

The text of Ezekiel makes the transforming effect of the vision vividly apparent. God speaks through Ezekiel and says, "Mortal, these bones are the whole house of Israel. They say, 'Our bones are dried up, and our hope is lost; we are cut off completely.' . . . I will put my Spirit within you, and you shall live . . . then you shall know that I, the Lord, have spoken and will act."

B. JESUS COMMUNICATED BY SHARING VISION. Recall the text from the Gospel of John: ". . . Look around you, and see how the fields are ripe for harvesting" (John 4:35). This is a clear invitation to see vividly the possibilities for ministry and mission. The same vision is quoted by both Matthew and Luke: "The harvest is plentiful, but the laborers are few." The vision of a ready harvest is a clear communication of a receptive people.

Jesus called followers by affirming and encouraging vision in words such as, "You are the salt of the earth; you are the light of the world."

In the parable of the sower, the attention of the listener is not to remain with the seed that falls upon the path and is eaten by the birds, the seed that falls upon rocky soil, the seed that sprouts in shallow soil that soon dries up, or the seed that is choked by the thorns. The focus is upon the seed that falls upon good soil and brings forth a hundredfold!

Parables of the lost coin, the lost sheep, and the lost son are clearly intended to create and to leave a vision of God's seeking those who feel abandoned, hopeless, lost, or separated from God. Each parable concludes with a picture of joy and the words, "Rejoice with me!"

C. THE HOLY SPIRIT ENERGIZES BY CREATING AND SUSTAINING VISION. Luke makes it abundantly clear in the Book of Acts that the presence of dreams and visions is one of the signs of the outpouring of God's Spirit. Peter preaches on the day of Pentecost (Acts 2). In response to those who accuse the apostles of being filled with new wine, he says, "Indeed, these are not drunk, as you suppose, for it is only nine o'clock in the morning. No, this is what was spoken through the prophet Joel:

> In the last days it will be, God declares,
> that I will pour out my Spirit upon all flesh,
> and your sons and your daughters shall prophesy,
> and your young men shall see visions,
> and your old men shall dream dreams.
> Even upon my slaves, both men and women,
> in those days I will pour out my Spirit;
> and they shall prophesy."
>
> (Acts 2:15-18)

The Book of Acts is a vivid reminder of the impact of vision upon the blindness of the church. The resistant Simon Peter is confronted in a vision with God's concern for Gentiles. In a vision Paul is invited to Macedonia. Through a vision Paul is sustained through the crisis of the storm in the great sea journey.

Paul's faithfulness during his ministry is summarized before authorities with the words, "I was not disobedient to the heavenly vision" (Acts 26:19). The apostolic posture was one of consistent, confident obedience to the vision of God's ultimate triumph in Jesus Christ.

D. THE NEW TESTAMENT CONCLUDES WITH A POWERFUL VISION that sustained the church during times of Roman persecution, with the certainty of God's victory over every defeat.

Without a powerful vision, the church ultimately reflects the hope-lessness and despair of the world around it. Such a church is drained and diverted from its mission and from the possibilities of life-transforming impact. Vision receptivity is thus one of the primary characteristics of the church of the future.

Imagine for a moment your congregation as vision-inspired and energized as you move into and beyond the year 2000. See your congregation as dynamic, hope-filled, and exciting. Your congregation responds not just to personal needs but to social issues and concerns.

You are moving forward in faithfulness to the God of hope. You are growing in obedience to the Great Commission of Jesus Christ to go into all the world and make disciples (Matthew 28:19-20). You are faithful to the work of the Holy Spirit in continuing the work of Jesus through the church. Your hope is contagious! Your congregation is a center of healing and of hope. Is such a picture possible? Is such a picture possible with the power of God?

E. THE APPROACH OF THE CALENDAR DATE 2000 CHALLENGES THE CHURCH to take seriously both *chronos* time and *kairos* time. This *chronos* date will have traumatic visibility for the next decade. Naisbitt and Aburdene write in *Megatrends 2000:* "For centuries a monumental symbolic date has stood for the future and what we make of it. In a few short years that future will be here. Already we have fallen under its influence. The year 2000 is operating like a giant magnet on humanity, reaching down into the '90s and intensifying the decade."[4]

The date is a constant reminder that short-range, "business as usual" planning is not adequate for the local church. Congregations are challenged to lean forward in faithful planning and visioning for the future. The year 2000 is larger than *chronos*. It points us to *kairos* possibilities. Faith, value, and meaning questions will be increasingly raised in the '90s. There will be times of unusual receptivity, which the church of Jesus Christ dares not ignore. Now is a good time to explore the power of biblical vision and to recover the potential of vision and dreams for personal and congregational life. What if the God who works through vision-receptive persons and groups extends to us the opportunity of joining in the formation of a new future for a new century? Imagine your congregation as joyously faithful to the God of hope. See your community of faith as a radiant center of healing and transformation. Is such a picture possible? Is such a picture possible with the power of God? Is it worth a major commitment of time and energy to move toward such vision-receptivity and responsiveness?

FOR REFLECTION,
DISCUSSION, AND REACTION

1. Give an illustration of the biblical claim: "Where there is no vision, the people perish."

2. Compare Ezekiel's task of preaching, described in the text, with the task of the pastor and church today.

3. Do you believe that the parables of the lost coin, the lost sheep, and the lost son create a vision? What do you see?

4. What kept Paul obedient to his "heavenly vision" (Acts 26:12-23)?

   Do we need this? How?

5. Share a vision you have experienced and your desire to be obedient to it.

6. Describe what you believe a vision-inspired church can and should do.

7. Try your hand at a rough draft of a one- or two-sentence "vision statement" for your local congregation. "It is the vision of _____(name)_____ congregation to

Share your "first impression" vision statement. The vision statement may be revised and refined at a later time. Don't worry about a perfect version here. First impression and initial concepts are important. Also, don't begin here to critique each other's first impression visions. Listen to and encourage one another, and look for the Spirit to be at work in your midst.

II FOCUSING ON BIBLICAL FOUNDATIONS FOR A POSTURE OF HOPE

Good news! You were born with the capacity for vision. By that, you now know we are talking about more than sight. Vision is the marvelous gift of God that enables us to see not only the "surface world," but also to picture and to envision depth, reality, and hidden potential to this world. Vision is essential for faithful response to God. Isaiah understood the importance of vision when he addressed the Jews caught in crushing Babylonian captivity. In secret home meetings, the exiles listened with eager anticipation as they heard these words read, "I am about to do a new thing; now it springs forth, do you not perceive it?" (Isaiah 43:19). The exiles went back into a world where everything looked just the same. Still, the words persisted, "I am about to do a new thing . . . do you not perceive it?"

A. OUR CULTURE UNDERSTANDS THE POWER OF THE VISUAL. The daily blitz of logos, symbols, news clips, and repeated commercials is almost overwhelming. Long before our modern use of graphics, the community of faith shared the reality of experience with God through pictures and stories. To understand vision, we must learn to "think Hebrew." The Hebrew vocabulary was limited. There were few words to communicate abstract concepts or ideas as found in Greek thought. The Greek vocabulary was far more complex. Greek thought tended to be analytical, logical, and sequential. It provided the foundation for the development of "Western" and "scientific" thought. Hebrew thought was more "earthy," focused upon describing people in highly dramatic, visual situations.

B. MUCH OF THE MATERIAL IN THE OLD TESTAMENT WAS MEANT TO BE SEEN. In the Old Testament, meaning comes through the visual.

In Osaka, Japan, at Expo '90, there was an Imax Theatre with a screen six stories high. The screen was shaped like the interior of a giant umbrella. Viewers were almost totally surrounded by the screen. A sophisticated Dolby sound system was synchronized very carefully with the film being projected.

1. *Imagine yourself seated in that great theatre.* Imagine looking up to an enormous screen and seeing some pictures. These pictures help us recall some of the scenes important in understanding biblical foundations for Vision 2000.

Take a moment. Relax. Close your eyes. Take a deep breath. Exhale slowly. Take another breath. Exhale slowly. Now focus upon the screen. See the enormous picture of an older man projected on the Imax screen. His face fills the screen. Every detail of his features is revealed. His beard is white. He has no teeth. There are many lines upon his face. He is bent, frail, and feeble. There is little hair on top of his head. He has a wife. She also is wrinkled, frail, and bent. Both move slowly. You think to yourself, "They have only a few remaining years. They should relax, take it easy, and enjoy life."

Watch them now as they enter a room. They begin to straighten up. Their heads and shoulders are held erect. They have smiles across their faces. They begin to move with greater energy. Their activity takes on an almost youthful vigor. They are almost laughing. What has happened? They are preparing for a journey. These two people appear to be far too old to attempt a lengthy journey. Why are they preparing for a journey? God has called them.

Imagine seeing these two older adults standing together in a little garden outside their house, holding hands. Abraham points to the stars and seems to be counting. We want to ask, "Excuse me, sir. What are you doing?" "We are counting stars." "Why are you counting stars?" "Because God has promised us that our descendants will be like the stars of the heavens and like the sand of the seashore—without number." And we are tempted to say, "Abraham! Sarah! Be reasonable. Have you talked to your doctor lately? Do you know the facts of life? Do you know that such a thing is absolutely impossible for someone of your age?" At least Abraham raised the question, "Can a child be born to a man who is a hundred years old? Can Sarah, who is ninety years old, bear a child?" (Genesis 17:17).

Still, the day came when the gates of Ur of Chaldees opened, and an older man and woman leaned forward into a vision, sustained only by the promise of God. At one point the narrator says of Abraham, "And he believed the Lord; and the Lord reckoned it to him as righteousness." As you watch that tiny caravan stretch out like a fragile thread across the desert, you see a response that is not forgotten. What a picture—an older couple leaning forward into an impossible vision.

Vision 2000 is never to be understood as a fantasy picture created by pious imagination. Vision 2000 is grounded in the reality of a vision-sharing God. Vision 2000 is a posture of leaning forward into the future that God prepares.

2. *Return to our Expo '90 theatre.* See the screen again. The scene changes. A younger man now appears on the screen. He is only 80 years old. His face is also projected so that it fills the six-story screen. His eyes are filled with terror. Lines of worry and anxiety move across his face. For a moment the camera catches his hands, which are twisting and turning in a moment of abject terror. Behind him viewers see a crowd of thousands of terrified slaves. Behind the slaves, Egyptian chariots approach with devastating certainty. It is apparent that the people and the leader do not have long to live.

Moses, who did not want the leadership position in the first place, prays. God answers, "Why do you cry out to me? Tell the Israelites to go forward" (Exodus 14:15). Only as Moses leans forward and begins to step forward is the way opened!

Do you remember the response of the people only a short time after this mighty act of deliverance? Their anger and resentment toward Moses because of the lack of their favorite Egyptian foods is a graphic reminder of the reality of vision resistance. Faithfulness to God in vision obedience inevitably releases a flood of vision resistance by those who are threatened by any change.

3. *Joshua also encountered vision resistance.* When ten of the twelve spies sent to investigate the land of Canaan brought back their negative, problem-exaggerating reports, the people responded in terror. Imagine the negative vision created by words such as, "We are not able to go up against this people, for they are stronger than we. . . . All the people that we saw in it are of great size. . . .To ourselves we seemed like grasshoppers, and so we seemed to them" (Numbers 13:31-33). Joshua had to wait forty years, as the people wandered in great circles in the desert wilderness. Finally, the time had come for a new vision, "Be strong and courageous; do not be frightened or dismayed, for the Lord your God is with you wherever you go." Joshua and Caleb leaned forward as the wilderness was finally left behind.

For other great examples of following a vision, consider Miriam, Ruth, Rahab, Hagar, and Esther. All of them leaned forward, led by a different way of seeing the future.

4. When the people had been scattered into Babylonian exile, *Ezekiel saw an amazing vision* of people catching fish on the shores of the Dead Sea. The people were there from En-gedi to En-eglaim,

on the shores of the most unlikely fishing place on the planet earth. How could anyone catch fish in this impossible place?

Ezekiel saw a stream flowing from beneath the altar of the temple in Jerusalem. Everyone who heard of this vision understood that the temple was already in ruins. Still, the stream flowed through the desolate Judean wilderness, with trees growing on each side of the river. "Their leaves will not wither nor their fruit fail, but they will bear fresh fruit every month, because the water for them flows from the sanctuary. Their fruit will be for food, and their leaves for healing" (Ezekiel 47:12). The water from the Dead Sea actually became fresh, because it was transformed by the power of the stream!

Ezekiel did not interpret the vision. He simply shared it and allowed it to speak for itself. He reported that God asked him only one question, "Mortal, *have you seen this?*" (Ezekiel 47:6). In other words, do you have the vision? Do you get the picture? Can you live by the picture?

C. EMPTY DREAMS AND FALSE VISIONS CAN CREATE PROB-LEMS. The prophets who communicated their visions of hope also repeatedly warned the community of faith about the deceptive and destructive nature of false visions and counterfeit dreams. The prophetic mission was to remind Israel of the destructive power of idolatry, injustice, and rebellion against God.

1. Jeremiah's terrible description of earth stands in shocking contrast to the vision of creation depicted in Genesis 1 and 2. Jeremiah's vision looks like a description of the earth as a nuclear wasteland— a total environmental disaster. It depicts, with unforgettable clarity, the effect of human rebellion and sin:

> I looked on the earth, and lo, it was waste and void;
>   and to the heavens, and they had no light.
> I looked on the mountains, and lo, they were quaking,
>   and all the hills moved to and fro.
> I looked, and lo, there was no one at all,
>   and all the birds of the air had fled.
> I looked, and lo, the fruitful land was a desert,
>   and all its cities were laid in ruins.
>   (Jeremiah 4:23-28)

Authentic vision must, at times, carry a shocking picture of the consequences of complacency and indifference. Jeremiah spoke often of the futility of the empty comfort of false dreams, saying, "They have treated the wound of my people carelessly, saying, 'Peace, peace,' when there is no peace. They acted shamefully, they committed abomination; yet they were not at all ashamed, they did not know how to blush" (Jeremiah 6:14-15; 8:11-12).

Vision without repentance and change is cheap vision and therefore destructive vision. Jeremiah confronted leaders who were tempted to share visions that were nothing more than their own pious wishes. Jeremiah understood that there are greedy prophets who exert pressure to produce "acceptable" visions.

> Thus says the Lord of hosts: Do not listen to the words of the prophets who prophesy to you; they are deluding you. They speak visions of their own minds, not from the mouth of the Lord. They keep saying to those who despise the word of the Lord, "It will be well with you"; and to all who stubbornly follow their own stubborn hearts, they say, "No calamity shall come upon you" (Jeremiah 23:16-17).

According to Jeremiah, there is peril in any vision that does not include repentance and deep commitment. Authentic vision is therefore never something that we imagine or create on our own. True vision is a gift from God who invites the community of faith to return to God. This genuine repentance and obedient faith before God is followed by the gift of a new vision of hope, which moves beyond judgment to grace.

> I have loved you with an everlasting love;
> therefore I have continued my faithfulness to you.
> Again I will build you, and you shall be built,
> O virgin Israel!
> Again you shall take your tambourines,
> and go forth in the dance of the merrymakers.
> Again you shall plant vineyards on the mountains of Samaria;
> the planters shall plant, and shall enjoy the fruit.
> (Jeremiah 31:3b-5)

2. The account of Micaiah, an earlier prophet of great integrity, demonstrates the tremendous pressure exerted by "court prophets" upon authentic prophets, to make their visions agree with what the king had already decided to do.

Get a mental picture of this court scene. The drama takes place in an open-air courtroom at a thrashing floor by the entrance to the gate of Samaria (1 Kings 22:10). Two kings, arrayed in their robes, are seated upon their thrones. The king of Israel says to his servants, "Do you know that Ramoth-gilead belongs to us, yet we are doing nothing to take it out of the hand of the king of Aram?" (1 Kings. 22:3). He then asked Jehoshaphat to go to battle with him. Jehoshaphat, King of Judah, answered, "I am as you are; my people are your people, my horses are your horses." Then Jehoshaphat added, "Inquire first for the word of the Lord."

The king of Israel was ready! Four-hundred court prophets were waiting to give the word the king wanted to hear. The prophets agreed, with no dissent. The unanimous verdict was given, "Go up; for the Lord will give it into the hand of the king."

The king of Judah hesitated. The agreement of 400 prophets made him nervous. He asked, "Is there no other prophet of the Lord here of whom we may inquire?" The king of Israel admitted to his neighbor, "There is still one other by whom we may inquire of the Lord, Micaiah son of Imlah; but I hate him, for he never prophesies anything favorable about me, but only disaster."

The command went out to summon Micaiah. The court prophets had already made horns of iron, and were presenting an exciting drama of how the enemy would be gored and destroyed. No wonder the messenger said to Micaiah, "Look, the words of the prophets with one accord are favorable to the king; let your word be like the word of one of them, and speak favorably." Micaiah answered, "As the Lord lives, whatever the Lord says to me, that I will speak" (1 Kings 22:14).

Standing before the kings on their thrones by the gates of Samaria, Micaiah not only spoke of the certainty of defeat in the proposed battle, but he also told the king about a lying spirit in his 400 prophets. Micaiah was then slapped and put into prison with reduced rations of bread and water.

3. Accurate vision-sharing has always been costly for authentic prophets and visionaries. Jesus warned about false prophets by saying, "Beware that no one leads you astray. For many will come in my name, saying, 'I am the Messiah!'" (Matthew 24:4-5).

> Then if anyone says to you, "Look! Here is the Messiah!" or "There he is!"—do not believe it. For false messiahs and false prophets will appear and produce great signs and omens, to lead astray, if possible, even the elect. Take note, I have told you beforehand. So, if they say to you, "Look! He is in the wilderness," do not go out. If they say, "Look! He is in the inner rooms," do not believe it (Matthew 24:23-26).

Jesus not only warns about the danger of false prophets with false visions, but he also warns against any attempt to set dates for God's mighty act in the culmination of earth's history. How amazing to read that even Jesus does not know the time of the final hour: "But about that day and hour no one knows, neither the angels of heaven, nor the Son, but only the Father" (Matthew 24:36). Luke reports the risen Christ saying to his followers in the upper room,

> It is not for you to know the times or periods that the Father has set by his own authority. But you will receive power when the Holy Spirit has come upon you; and you will be my witnesses in Jerusalem, in all Judea and Samaria, and to the ends of the earth (Acts 1:7-8).

In light of these very clear warnings, we might appropriately ask, How then can some modern writers claim to know more than Jesus by actually setting the date when he will return? Why do so many who want to take the Bible literally avoid a literal interpretation of these clear passages? Please, give us no more dates, popular writers! Please, offer no more visions that claim the year 2000 as the date of the second coming of Jesus Christ. We shall later develop our thesis that the year 2000 does have the power of both *chronos* and *kairos* time for people on our planet. Let's be clear right now, however, that every temptation to identify that date with the end of earth's history must be avoided. Calendar abuse is false prophecy! It is a mistake.

FOR REFLECTION, DISCUSSION, AND REACTION

1. Did you sit in the great theater and "see" the story of Abraham and Sarah unfold? Was it real to you? What made it real? How can we use this method in Bible reading/study for vision formation?

2. Joshua's "vision resisters" numbered 10 to 2. Is this true in our church today? What was the result of the Joshua vote (Numbers 14:1-9)?

3. Can you envision a "stream" flowing from your church, from your altar, out into the community? How deep is it and what difference does it make?

4. Discuss some "inauthentic (false) visions" of today. Are they easily identified?

5. Are you willing to say with Micaiah, "Whatever the Lord says to me, that I will speak"? Do you believe this is what your church wants this Team to do?

6. Is your congregation preoccupied with trying to predict the date of Jesus' second coming? Whether or not your congregation knows this temptation, describe how such a preoccupation could interfere with a truly biblical approach to the future.

III | THE VISION OF JESUS

A. ALL DISCUSSION OF VISION MUST ULTIMATELY BE BROUGHT BEFORE THE VISION OF JESUS. Where do you find this vision? It is of course presumptuous to assert that we can speak with absolute finality about the vision carried by Jesus Christ for his ministry. Still, a number of clues are given in the Gospels that help us see the vision that judges all visions.

Jesus began his ministry in the power of the Spirit. The Gospel of Luke presents a picture of Jesus as the fulfillment of the expectation that goes all the way back to the story of Adam and Eve. Jesus was, therefore, the fulfillment of prophecy and the sign of the new age of the Spirit. Readers of the Gospel of Luke hear John the Baptist saying, "I baptize you with water; but one who is more powerful than I is coming; I am not worthy to untie the thong of his sandals. He will baptize you with the Holy Spirit and fire" (Luke 3:16). Jesus is the one who pours out the Spirit. ". . . He has poured out this that you both see and hear" (Acts 2:33).

Jesus was baptized with ordinary people, and as he "was praying, the heaven was opened, and the Holy Spirit descended upon him in bodily form like a dove. And a voice came from heaven, 'You are my Son, the Beloved; with you I am well pleased'" (Luke 3:21-22).

Jesus' victory over temptation was in the power of the Spirit (Luke 4:1-13). The temptation experience of Jesus shows us his rejection of three false visions:

a) The vision of a powerful leader who would gain a following by providing food for the hungry multitudes.

b) The vision of a miraculous leader who would astonish the multitudes by spectacular miracles.

c) The vision of a compromising leader who would gain victory without suffering, by special arrangements with Satan.

The rejection of these false visions brought an even greater certainty of the "power of the Spirit" with which Jesus returned to Galilee.

Jesus' first sermon in Nazareth set forth a vision that was to guide his earthly ministry.

He stood up to read, and the scroll of the prophet Isaiah was given to him. He unrolled the scroll and found the place where it was written:

"The Spirit of the Lord is upon me,
because he has anointed me to bring good news to the poor.
He has sent me to proclaim release to the captives
and recovery of sight to the blind,
to let the oppressed go free,
to proclaim the year of the Lord's favor."

And he rolled up the scroll, gave it back to the attendant, and sat down. . . . Then he began to say to them, "Today this scripture has been fulfilled in your hearing" (Luke 4:16b-21).

Jesus' vision looked beyond the *status quo*. He was continually reaching out to and declaring the love of God for people whom others had rejected. The early church could well remember how this brought Jesus into conflict with some of the customs and conventions of his day. Luke wanted his readers to see Jesus as he touched the "untouchable" leper and responded to his plea: "Lord, if you choose, you can make me clean." Jesus responded immediately by saying, "I do choose. Be made clean" (Luke 5:12-13). The rest of the Gospel of Luke gives us pictures of how Jesus carried out this vision in his ministry. In this vision people can see themselves being touched and transformed.

Of course, there were no stained glass windows or paintings in churches for hundreds of years. People carried pictures within, and they returned again and again to hear Luke's story in order to renew their vision of Jesus touching the poor, the outcast, the lepers, the woman with the flow of blood, and a widow from Nain.

The church visualized the response of ordinary people to Jesus. Four men carried a friend to Jesus and lowered him through a hole in the roof. A Samaritan leper returned to give thanks. An officer in the hated Roman army of occupation sent messengers telling Jesus that he did not need to come to his home to heal the sick slave. Jesus needed only to say the word, and the servant would be healed (Luke 7:2-10). The blind beggar named Bartimaeus followed Jesus, glorifying God, and he inspired others to do the same (Luke 18:35-43). A chief tax collector gave half of his goods to the poor and restored fourfold those whom he had deceived and defrauded (Luke 19:2-9).

Had Luke known the story of the outcast Samaritan woman who won her village to Christ (John 4:1-41), he would certainly have included it. Luke not only would have wanted to help the church formulate its vision of one who talked to a Samaritan outcast, but he also would have wanted the church to see the power of the witness of one excited person. In Luke, the vision of Jesus is known fully only in the response of people to him. Always the vision is consistent with the text read in the Nazareth synagogue.

B. IN THE BOOK OF ACTS, LUKE MAKES IT VIVIDLY CLEAR THAT THE VISION OF JESUS CONTINUES IN THE LIFE AND PREACHING OF THE CHURCH. Authentic vision is always given by God and carried by ordinary people into the community of faith by the power of the Holy Spirit.

The church always read the Gospels in the light of the resurrection of Jesus and the outpouring of the Holy Spirit. This led to a joyous certainty of the continuity of the ministry of Jesus. What Jesus did in the Gospels he continues to do through the Spirit in the life of the church. The Gospels are never to be seen as merely a report of what happened. Rather, they are a celebration of what is still happening! The teaching sections of the Gospels are not reports of what Jesus taught. They are clues to what Jesus is still teaching.

The central motivating theme of Jesus' teaching was the "kingdom of God." Jesus spoke of the kingdom more than eighty times in the Gospels. The present and coming reign of God appears in Jesus' teachings and conversations more than any other concern. The parables focus upon the kingdom of God with phrases such as "The kingdom of God is like. . . ."

Luke wanted his readers to understand that the kingdom of God was the central message of the resurrected Lord as well. In the Book of Acts, Luke writes, "After his suffering he presented himself alive to them by many convincing proofs, appearing to them during forty days and speaking about the kingdom of God" (Acts 1:3).

Jesus resisted the interpretation of the kingdom as ethnic or national imperialism. He rejected the idea that God comes to restore the ancient boundaries and past glories to Israel. Therefore, it is amazing to read that after this additional teaching time of forty days, the first question asked of Jesus revealed a total misunderstanding of the kingdom of God. "Lord, is this the time when you will restore the kingdom to Israel?" (Acts 1:6). Imagine how frustrating it would be to teach a forty-day seminar on a theme and then to have the first question reveal a total misunderstanding of the content of the seminar!

In keeping with the whole tenor of his ministry, Jesus' answer looks beyond a narrow, self-serving vision to the future of the church in the power of the Spirit:

It is not for you to know the times or periods that the Father has set by his own authority. But you will receive power when the Holy Spirit has come upon you; and you will be my witnesses in Jerusalem, in all Judea and Samaria, and to the ends of the earth (Acts 1:7-8).

The full scope of Jesus' vision of the kingdom is seen only as we read the Gospels and the Book of Acts together. The early Christians understood that Jesus wanted them to see the continuation of his ministry in the reality and development of theirs. Jesus promised the outpouring of his Spirit in order to create the church, in order for the church to witness to him, in order for the church to become a sign of the kingdom. In the ministry of the church—in its acts of compassion for the poor; in its acts of justice before oppressive structures; in its acts of devotion in prayer and scripture reading; and in its acts of worship in preaching, baptism, and the Lord's Supper—the early Christians recognized their continuing witness to the ministry of Jesus and to the vision of the kingdom that he inaugurated.

Jesus did not limit his vision of the kingdom to his own earthly life. Nor did he limit it to the group of his earliest followers. Rather, he promised that the church in the power of the Spirit would witness to him "to the ends of the earth." In obedience to Jesus, the church is called to be, and increasingly to become, the sign of God's reign and future victory. Following Jesus' lead, the church is not the kingdom, but it is the sign of God's future reign over all things.

C. THE CHURCH CONTINUES TO RESPOND TO JESUS' VISION. Like the earliest Christians, the church throughout history has been challenged and energized by entering again and again into the vision of Jesus. Whenever this has occurred in a remarkable way, moreover, the church has let its own imagination come alive—to see Jesus, and the response of ordinary people to him, in ever new ways. For those who would participate in Jesus' vision, imagination has always been required.

Take, for example, the story of the paralytic and his friends. Listeners with imagination place themselves in that setting as the four men come around the last corner to see that every window and every door is filled in the home where Jesus is teaching. If we truly "get into" the story, we can sense the urgency and expectation of the carriers as they find the outside stairway and take courage to see new possibilities for accomplishing their goal. What kind of determination does it take to start removing tiles from the roof of another person's house in order to gain access?

Lowering the man through the hole requires imagination. The men had to unwind and tie their sashes together, tying the cloth to the ends of the pallet. With one slip of a bad knot, their friend would fall! Their persistence and faith were not ignored by Jesus. When the paralytic was lowered, Jesus said to him, "Friend, your sins are forgiven you" (Luke 5:20).

The early church recalled with special joy Jesus' insistence that he not only had authority to pronounce the words of forgiveness, but also to say, ". . . Stand up and take your bed and go to your home" (Luke 5:24). The man took up his bed and went home glorifying God. Luke reports the response of the people: "Amazement seized all of them, and they glorified God and were filled with awe . . ." (Luke 5:26). Later, the church heard the story with imagination. They shared in the vision of Jesus. Faithful participation in the vision of Jesus brings that response again and again as the story is told and retold.

The conversation with the outcast woman by the well in Samaria is another example. This story had helped the church formulate its vision in response to the vision of Jesus by reaching out to include all persons. In the woman's excited word of witness to her village, the church has seen the possibilities of communicating the gospel vision across seemingly impossible barriers. By telling and retelling the story, the church has been continually challenged and energized by the power of Jesus' vision. In every generation, the church has listened and understood that Jesus' vision is larger than once imagined.

Jesus' vision of release to the captives, good news to the poor, and healing and forgiveness to restore broken relationships with God and between people is given to the Spirit-empowered church. This is the vision Peter announced on the day of Pentecost—a new day of salvation, healing, deliverance, shalom, and restoration. The vision is the same as that which Paul saw for the future of God's people throughout the world: "So if anyone is in Christ, there is a new creation: everything old has passed away; see, everything has become new!" (2 Corinthians 5:17). Such a vision must be shared.

FOR REFLECTION, DISCUSSION, AND REACTION

1. What was John the Baptist's vision at the time of Jesus' baptism (Luke 3:1-18)?

2. How would you describe the false visions with which Jesus wrestled at the time of his temptation (Luke 4:1-13)?

   How did he handle them?

   Are such visions still with us? How?

3. Paraphrase in your own words some of the "clues" that help us understand Jesus' vision for his ministry.

4. What should Jesus' vision of the kingdom mean for the church today? Name some areas or issues where the church is called today to continue Jesus' vision.

5. Were Jesus' visions quickly understood? Will our visions be quickly understood and accepted? What is required to bring them to reality?

IV | YESTERDAY'S DREAMS— TODAY'S REALITIES

Dreams may be forgotten as quickly as they are dreamed, or they may become visions that possess the dreamer. When this happens, they refuse to subside no matter what obstacles arise. What makes this happen? Doubtless much depends upon the intensity of the dream and the determination of the dreamer.

We now take a look at some dreams that possessed their dreamers and that, despite the obstacles and hardships involved, became realities. These may encourage, inspire, and illuminate the reader. Each dreamer has a different story to tell and to be remembered as your church begins to fashion and form its dream.

A. MARY McLEOD BETHUNE DREAMED A SCHOOL AND A COLLEGE FOR YOUNG AFRICAN-AMERICAN WOMEN INTO REALITY.

Mary McLeod Bethune, born in 1875 in South Carolina, the fifteenth child of slave parents, was possessed by a dream. Early in her life she had fondly picked up a book in a landowner's home, only to be told, "Put that book down; you can't read." Instinctively Bethune knew this was what made such a difference between her and white children. She wanted more than anything else to know how to read.

The Board of Missions for Freedman opened the door of opportunity, and Mary eagerly ran the five miles from her "home" education to a "school" education. Later the tithe of a seamstress in Denver, Colorado, opened the next opportunity for learning and she continued until she had completed her formal training at the Moody Bible Institute in Chicago, Illinois.

The dream of going to Africa as a missionary to teach children led her at age twenty to make application with the Mission Board of the Presbyterian Church. Her answer, however, was a bitter disappointment. They replied, "No openings for a Negro missionary in Africa."

One door had closed, but if she were denied the dream of teaching black children in Africa, she would not be denied the dream of teaching black girls in her Southland. The intensity of the dream and the determination of the dreamer made the difference.

Can you see her coming to Daytona Beach, Florida, to start her own school for Negro girls? She had only $1.50 to put down when she rented a two-story, frame building for $11.00 a month. Mr. Williams, the owner, said she looked as if she could be trusted for the balance. Bethune then scraped together the meager furniture with which to open her school. Five girls were present on the first day.

Can you see her now, envisioning her own property; finding a suitable plot of land, 50' × 100', which cost $250.00; inviting James M. Gamble of Proctor and Gamble of Cincinnati, Ohio, who wintered in Daytona Beach, to be a "trustee" of her school and to be her "Chairman of the Board of Trustees"? She had learned of him through his gardener, and he was described as being "a very kind man." She wrote a note to Gamble and asked for an appointment to talk with him about a school. Rackham Holt describes the event in her memorable biography, *Mary McLeod Bethune.*

> She announced herself, "I'm Mary McLeod Bethune." "Oh, you are the one who wrote me about your school. I thought you were a white woman. Won't you come in."

> The real kind man led her into the library and asked her to be seated while she amplified her letter. She spoke of the imperative need for instruction for Negro girls.

> "I am not coming to you for money, Mr. Gamble, but to ask you for your personal interest in the work I have it in my mind to do. . . . Mr. Gamble, I am asking you to be a trustee."

> "A trustee of what?"

> "A trustee of a dream. This is my dream—this school. Will you give me some advice right now? Is it foolish to attempt this school on my part, or is it a dream that may come true?"

> Mr. Gamble was impressed enough to say, "I'll at least come over and see what you are doing. Will Wednesday be alright?"

> Mrs. Bethune invited a few other representative men whom she hoped would become members of her Board. She included the Mayor, an outstanding Realtor and two Negro pastors. Her students, who numbered about 20 at that time, were grouped on the stairway where they conducted the exercises of recitations and songs. She then told the visitors the story of her own life, and with characteristic gestures swept her hands over the girls. She said they could accomplish great things if they were given the opportunity.

> She then proceeded, "I have asked you gentlemen here for a special reason—to establish a Board of Trustees." Mr. Gamble was the first to announce, "I'll be on the Board. I will accept that trust." All

accepted the position of trustees, and Mr. Gamble agreed to serve as Chairman.[5]

Mary McLeod Bethune was now on her way to a life of distinguished service, not only in the field of education, but also in government and in work through the NAACP. Three presidents sought her help in federal positions.

On the fiftieth anniversary, that first small plot of ground had expanded to a 36-acre campus. The two-story frame building had become nineteen buildings with a plant valued in the millions of dollars. The five little girls had grown to an enrollment of 1,300, and thousands of black girls had gone into life with a preparation they could never have had if it had not been for Mary's dream.

B. SUNDO KIM OF SEOUL, KOREA, DREAMED A CHURCH WITH 50,000 MEMBERS INTO REALITY.

Dr. Kim is a man with a vision. He is pastor of Kwang-Lim (Burning Bush Church) in Seoul, Korea. Years ago the congregation was located in a building surrounded by factories and industrial buildings. A few miles away on the other side of the Han River, great high-rise buildings were being constructed to house the exploding population of this dynamic city. Dr. and Mrs. Kim began to search for property for a new church building to serve people where they were living.

The Kims found an ideal site for the new church in a pear orchard that literally was surrounded by buildings of the new city. Inquiries revealed that the property was not for sale. It was held by several members of a family that was not interested in the church. The Kims were not discouraged by the owners' unwillingness to sell. Day after day they returned to the old pear orchard to kneel in the mud and pray. This continued for thirty days. They prayed that God would bless them with guidance so that they could have leadership in building a church that would glorify God and share the gospel of Jesus Christ.

After praying for thirty days, Kim went back to the owners of the property. They were still unwilling to sell. On Sunday morning, Kim shared his vision with the entire Kwang-Lim congregation. The people's hearts were touched by the vision of reaching unchurched persons for Jesus Christ in this new location. Kim invited members of the church to join him in marching around the property, praying that God would help them in their mission. Members responded. They gathered on the vacant lot and began to march around the property, praying and singing as they marched. Like Joshua and the people of Israel of old, they dared to believe that the impossible could be accomplished.

Something happened! The owners suddenly reconsidered their refusal to sell. Disgruntled family members had changed their minds. Now the family was in total agreement to sell the property—and to sell it at a favorable price to the church.

The dream has grown beyond anyone's expectations. Now, a beautiful new sanctuary with an excellent educational building stands on the site of the old pear orchard. Today's congregation has grown to more than 50,000 members. Each Sunday four worship services are held with approximately 5,000 worshipers packed into the sanctuary for each service. The church has more than 3,000 neighborhood Bible study sharing groups (Wesleyan Class Meetings) meeting weekly. At the early morning prayer meeting, which occurs each morning of the year, more than 500 people study the scriptures and pray. The Kwang-Lim congregation continues its focus upon prayer with the completion of a beautiful new prayer retreat center that can accommodate more than 1,200 persons.

The Kwang-Lim congregation has a dynamic ministry, paying pastors' salaries in Poland and in other eastern European countries. Ministries have expanded to China, Japan, and the United States. Every year, hundreds of pastors come to Kwang-Lim for a spiritual renewal experience in a "Vision and Growth Seminar." The Kwang-Lim worship service is broadcast not only across Korea, but also to Hawaii and the western states of the USA.

A young convert from Buddhism said to a visiting pastor from the United States, "I am so happy since I found this church. My friend invited me. I never knew about Jesus. I invited Jesus into my heart. I have found a new life in Jesus Christ." The Kwang-Lim congregation is an exciting demonstration of the power of yesterday's dreams and visions that have become today's realities.

C. ELIJAH SHIMBURA, A MUSLIM NATIVE OF KENYA, AFRICA, DREAMED OF BECOMING A MINISTER AND WINNING THE FIRST OF THE MASAI TRIBE TO CHRIST.

Elijah Shimbura was born into a Moslem family in the hot, mosquito-infested Tana River area of Kenya, East Africa. He says that when he was a boy, he would climb the trees to watch lions stalk and kill their prey. When his family moved to Mombasa along the Indian Ocean coast, Shimbura met a Christian missionary. He had been warned about the desire of Christians to impose their faith upon others. To his amazement, this missionary was different! He became a friend. The missionary offered no pressure or strained effort to force other beliefs upon the Moslem lad. Shimbura noticed something in the older man's life that he admired.

One day he asked the secret of the man's peace and happiness. The missionary told him about Jesus. He told the young Moslem that Jesus was mentioned in the Koran. He pointed out that the Koran actually teaches that Jesus was a holy man, a respected prophet. Eventually, the missionary shared with Shimbura a copy of the New Testament. The young Moslem read with absolute amazement the story of the ministry, death, and resurrection of Jesus. He told his friend that he wanted to become a follower of Jesus. When he announced to his family that he wanted to be baptized, he was beaten so badly that he bears to this day the scars from the wounds that were inflicted upon him.

After becoming Christian, Elijah Shimbura felt God's call to the ministry of preaching. After receiving training in a seminary at Kaaga, which is a short distance from snowcapped Mount Kenya, he sensed again God's call. This time, he was called to share the gospel with the Masai people. The Masai, fiercely independent people, had stubbornly resisted all efforts by missionaries to evangelize them. Elijah Shimbura had a vision of the Masai actually becoming followers of Jesus Christ.

The young man was sent by his bishop to the "West Kenya Mission." That mission assignment included 340 congregations scattered among the Kisii and Luo tribes. The mission bordered land of the Masai. When he ventured into Masai territory, they laughed at him. He was so much shorter than they were. They called him a word which means "sissy" or "wimp" because he did not carry a spear or knife but only a walking stick and a Bible.

Shimbura kept praying for the Masai people. One day, while he was preaching in a small Kisii congregation bordering the Masai tribe, several Masai elders walked into the church. They later reported that they felt their God calling them to learn about Jesus. When they heard the dynamic, passionate preaching, they responded immediately by saying, "This is our church! We know about God; we want you to tell us about Jesus."

Gradually, piece by piece, the vision became a reality. Plans were drawn up for the first Masai church building. A pastor and laypeople from a church in Washington State caught the vision and volunteered to help. Finally the day came when the new building was completed. The bishop of Kenya was present and joined Shimbura and the volunteers from Washington State for the baptism of the first Masai. These converts were baptized and received into membership. Among them was a young couple, John and Lucy Musa-Kenya, who had already been serving as unbaptized missionaries to help lead the tribe to Jesus Christ.

One of the laypersons from Washington State who had helped build the church said, "I'll never forget that moment when the water of baptism mingled with the tears of the Masai. Their faces were radiant! I saw Jesus in the faces of the Masai!"

The vision continues. The church roof was designed so that rainwater would be collected and stored. The infant morality rate has dropped dramatically. The church is used daily for a school and clinic as well as for worship on Sundays. New congregations are being established with Masai leadership—because one young Moslem obeyed the vision!

D. LARRY MELLON DREAMED OF BECOMING A PHYSICIAN LIKE ALBERT SCHWEITZER.

The most amazing thing about dreams is that they captivate not only the dreamer, but even years later the recounting of the dream can captivate others who in turn dream similar dreams. They in turn captivate others to follow their dreams.

Nowhere is this more vividly demonstrated than in the life of Albert Schweitzer who, at the age of twenty-one as a university student, felt he could not accept his life of privilege and opportunity without committing himself to service. This was a *kairos* experience in *chronos* time.

He allowed himself nine more years to complete his studies in theology and to perfect his tremendous talents as an organist, as a builder of organs, and as a writer and lecturer in theology. Then, when he was thirty, he enrolled in medical school and upon graduation went to Lambarene in Africa to establish his own hospital.

Many years later, in 1947, Larry Mellon, an heir of the Andrew Mellon banking, oil, and aluminum fortune, read a *Life* magazine story about Schweitzer. He was then thirty-seven years old, married, and living on a ranch in Texas. The article described Schweitzer as the world's greatest man, and Mellon's heart raced as he read of this jungle doctor's accomplishments. Schweitzer's dream now became Mellon's dream, only to be cast in a different locale.

In the fall 1989 issue of *Pursuits* magazine Teo Furtado tells how Mellon, without a previous college degree, completed his pre-med studies in fifteen months. He was accepted at the prestigious Tulane Medical School, and in three years he and his wife were off to Haiti to erect their hospital in the Artibonite Valley where 250,000 people had only one small dispensary to care for their health needs.

Gwen, his wife, supervised the construction of the hospital, while Mellon completed his studies. Then together they opened the Albert Schweitzer Hospital. The workload was overpowering, and some physicians could not handle it. One doctor, in handing in his resignation said, "What you're doing here is trying to empty an ocean of misery with a teacup."[6]

When Mellon's work became recognized, money, medicine, and physicians began to arrive. By 1960 Mellon turned over the administration of the hospital to others, and he devoted himself to seeking to correct causes of the illnesses. "For more than 12 years, he capped springs, dug ditches, and laid PVC pipe, thereby reducing the risk of typhoid or dysentery. . . . As a result of his efforts, the number of life-threatening diseases dropped in the valley."[7] Mellon had now inspired others to take up the work where he left off.

He died in 1989 at the age of seventy-nine, but the dreams of these two dreamers still live and doubtlessly will inspire others in generations to come, who will find their hearts racing and their minds expanding as they dream their dreams.

Can you begin even now to dream such a dream for your church, for the work of God's kingdom, and for the opportunity to reach out and meet the most apparent needs of your community? Think how far-reaching this may be by the year 2000!

E. NOT ALL DREAMS HAVE THE SAME TIMETABLE.

Recently the Hubble Space Telescope, first dreamed of in 1962 and launched in 1990, had a problem known as "eye trouble." This problem tested the ingenuity of the telescope's engineers. The vision for the telescope is to give humankind its greatest opportunity to look back toward the time when our universe was a cosmic egg, smaller than a pinhead, before the "big bang" of God's creative act occurred. This would tell the story of quasars, which release as much energy in a single second as our sun does in 10,000 years. However, this giant solar telescope was launched with a faulty mirror, and, until its repair in early 1994, its usefulness was seriously impaired.

The dream lives on, however. With perseverance, NASA scientists have been able to begin unlocking secrets that have been unknown since the creation of the world.

Likewise, the great inventor Thomas Edison had to practice persistence. Edison dreamed of the incandescent lamp but had to conduct thousands of experiments before he succeeded in finding the way that worked. The important thing was that the dream did not die with his failures.

We, too, are confronted with the necessity of being tested to see if we have the perseverance and the complete commitment necessary to bring our dreams into fruition. Many of us are products of the "instant" age. We have instant coffee, microwave ovens, instant electronic buying and banking operations, and many other instant products.

The pressing question on the minds of the disciples after Jesus' resurrection was, "Lord, is this the time when you will restore the kingdom to Israel?" This was their greatest dream. They wanted it— now. "Lord, will you establish your reign *now,* so we won't have to wait (or work) any longer? We have already waited three years."

Jesus' response brought the work of the kingdom into focus for all time. We are not to know the exact time or the exact season when our dreams for the kingdom are to be realized. On the other hand, we need not grow weary in our well-doing, for Jesus has promised to provide the power, the presence, and the spirit necessary to keep us faithful. Most of God's dreams for the kingdom are not of the "instant" variety. Most are hammered out on the anvil of life's greatest needs— needs that have been in existence for a long time and do not have quick-fix solutions. Fortunately, however, we can learn as much from the developmental period of our visions as we can from their earliest conception or their coming fulfillment.

When ordinary people are gripped by a great vision and open their lives to the power of the Holy Spirit, miracles still happen. The future is still open for dream-inspired and dream-motivated persons and congregations who pour the passion of their committed lives into the realization of God's dreams and visions.

FOR REFLECTION, DISCUSSION, AND REACTION

1. Distinguish between a *dream* and a *vision* as these terms are used in this study.

2. What impresses you most about the dreams of Mary McLeod Bethune?

3. Can you name others who have dreamed like this?

4. What was the most interesting thing to you about the dreams of each of the following:

   Sundo Kim—

   Elijah Shimbura—

   Larry Mellon—

5. What is the greatest dream you have ever had for your part in the kingdom of God?

6. What do dreams in this chapter suggest to you about the possibilities for realizing your own?

2 STEPS TO TAKE AT THIS TIME

You are now at least four sessions into your Vision 2000 experience! We are hopeful that the biblical studies, the review of yesterday's dreams as today's realities, and other preparations have produced a very real sense of excitement and anticipation.

The special objective at this point is to involve the whole congregation again in the visioning process and to prepare the Vision 2000 Team for "Developing and Experiencing the Vision" (Session 7). Along with the original commissioning of the Vision 2000 Team, this is the second formal opportunity for the congregation to participate. Specifically, the plan is to invite the congregational members themselves to envision in a preliminary way one of the concrete goals that the Team will be considering in the weeks to come. The goal selected for this "envisioning experience" is that of "Average Attendance in Worship and Sunday School by the Year 2000." Before moving to a description of this experience, it will be helpful to understand the pattern now developing.

VISION 2000 CONTINUES TO AND THROUGH THE YEAR 2000
The steps you have taken so far and the steps you are taking right now will be the springboard of decisions, actions, and activities that will continue into the next century. You and your governing body will determine which dreams will be developed and on what timetable they will happen.

As your dreams unfold and as you move toward the key celebrations of the year 2000, special attention should be given to anticipatory celebrations along the way—as dreams and visions are launched, as they achieve some success, as they reach climactic points, and as they are completed or achieved. Keep keen interest alive in the anticipation and achievement of as many "visions" as possible, and inaugurate special services for the high festival days of the church calendar to further highlight the working of God's Spirit in your congregation. This will have particular relevance to the "measurable goals" that the Vision 2000 Team will present as the result of its work in Session 7.

As you approach the year 2000 and as you move into the next century, the key focal point for each year will be Pentecost Sunday. This day should be highlighted on the church calendar and designated as the

"Vision 2000 Day of Receptivity" for God's dreams for your congregation. This annual day will keep alive the dreams now being formulated. It will open the door to the new dreams and visions that will emerge. The day will provide opportunity to update the Vision 2000 Team membership and the projected schedule. Although the Vision 2000 program does not have to be launched at any one time of the year, once it has been launched, the Pentecost date is of prime importance each year.

PREPARING FOR THE VISION

As a Team and as a congregation, it is time to prepare for the vision focus on "Average Attendance in Morning Worship and Sunday School by the Year 2000." As mentioned above, this is an opportunity to involve the whole congregation in the visioning process in a way that anticipates and paves the way for the work of the Team in the weeks to come. Each member of the congregation will be given a Vision 2000 Card to fill out. (See Appendix A, page 92, for a sample of this card, which you may copy.) The members of the congregation will be asked to lean forward into the future with bold faith by indicating what they believe an inspired goal for average attendance in worship and Sunday school can be by the year 2000. The responses will be tabulated. The results will become part of the information that the Vision 2000 Team uses in its own charge to set measurable goals for ministry into the next century. Here are the steps that should be taken in order to make this envisioning experience an effective event.

1. Plan this "Envisioning Sunday" to take place two weeks before the Team will be working on the second part of Session 7.

2. Prior to Envisioning Sunday, the pastor should:

   a. Describe again in the church bulletin and/or newspaper the work of the Vision 2000 Team and its progress thus far.

   b. Invite the congregation to support the Team by joining in the envisioning experience as described here. (See suggested copy for the church bulletin and/or newspaper in Appendix A, page 92.)

   c. Explain that the responses of Envisioning Sunday will become part of the Team's visioning process and that the congregation can anticipate a report of measurable goals in the weeks to come.

   d. Give the congregation the statistical data for worship and Sunday school average attendance for the last twenty years. (A format for presenting this data is given in Appendix A, page 93.)

3. On Envisioning Sunday, you should follow these steps:

   a. Have the Vision 2000 Cards prepared in advance. The envisioning experience should take place just prior to the normal time for receiving the offering.

b. As the cards are being passed out, the pastor should explain what is being done and why it is being done. This will avoid anyone filling in the cards before the prayer for vision is offered.

c. When all have their cards, the pastor should be prepared to lead the congregation in the envisioning experience, asking all members to "see" the number of people they believe God wishes this congregation to have in attendance by the year 2000. (The suggested newspaper copy in Appendix A also provides an inspiring script for the envisioning experience). This experience culminates in the offering of the "Envisioning Prayer" (Appendix A, page 93).

d. After the Envisioning Prayer has been offered, members write down their "faith numbers" and pass the cards to the center aisle where they are collected by the ushers before the offering plates are passed.

e. The Vision 2000 chairperson will have appointed two persons to receive these cards. These persons will take the cards, note the highs and the lows, categorize the cards in whatever way they wish, determine the average of the numbers submitted, and have this information ready for the Team at its meeting for Session 7.

4. In all of this, keep thinking of how you can prepare for and/or follow up the envisioning experience in ways that maximize the congregation's growing involvement in the total process.

V STEPS IN PREPARATION FOR THE VISION

A. RECOGNIZE THE CHARACTERISTICS OF NO-VISION CONGREGATIONS. Are you wearing glasses to read these words? How many in your Vision 2000 group wear glasses? When you first got glasses, you were not blind. Instead, in all probability, you were experiencing some visual distortion. Perhaps you were near-sighted or far-sighted or had some astigmatism. Can you remember the first time you saw the world around you through corrective lenses? You saw something out there that was not blurred. The world came into beautiful new focus! One youth with new glasses exclaimed, "Wow! I never knew the trees had so many individual leaves! I can even see what the teacher is writing on the board now."

Congregations need vision. Without vision, congregations tend to develop several problems.

1. No-vision congregations become complacent, stagnant, and boring. Hundreds of congregations simply exist. A new coat on display in a Midwestern shopping mall had beside it this description: "This coat captures beautifully that informal air of complete unconcern!" That motto is fine for a coat, but not good for a church!

In his book *My Six Convicts*, Donald Wilson refers to the study of personalities of prisoners at Fort Leavenworth Penitentiary in Kansas. One of the prisoners is named Weary Willie. He has committed no major crime, but is taking the rap for a smarter criminal. Day after day, he shuffles along the prison corridors. He has never done any real harm, but he has never done any good either.[8] Without vision, congregations tend to stoop, droop, and shuffle through endless days of monotony and boredom. While they do not do a lot of damage, neither do these congregations accomplish great good for the kingdom of God. Some congregations just bore people to death, leaving them lukewarm and apathetic.

According to a story, a man died in church. Ushers called the 911 emergency number. The ambulance arrived. The paramedics could not find the dead man. In fact, they carried out half the congregation before they found the man who was actually dead. Vision brings life! Without vision, a church experiences lethal lethargy and devastating apathy.

Inspiring vision helps a congregation retain its youthful energy, excitement, and commitment. Without vision, congregations become like barnacles. The barnacle begins its life as a free-swimming creature in saltwater. Eventually it fastens itself to a rock or a piling, builds a hard shell around itself, and spends the rest of its life kicking food into its mouth.

2. Congregations with no vision are never grasped by awe and gratitude for the wonder of God's gracious gifts. I once read an amazing story of a man who suddenly regained his sight after thirty years of blindness. He was unable to describe the way he felt. The world was a new place for him. Streets, automobiles, skyscrapers— everything had changed in thirty years.

The picture of his wife he had carried in his mind was of a young girl in her twenties, dark-haired, and beautiful. When his sight returned, he saw a kindly-faced woman he did not know, yet he did know it was his wife. Her hair was gray, and she had changed, but to him, she was more beautiful than he remembered.

After several days of sight, he still couldn't sleep at night. When he saw flowers for the first time in thirty years, he hung around them like a bee.

Authentic vision is like that. We often see, but do not see.

One of this book's authors remembers vividly the first time he saw tropical fish and coral through a face mask: I was introduced to snorkeling by my friend Larry, who was serving as pastor of First Church in Honolulu. He took me to a magnificent place called Hanama Bay on Oahu. On the surface, the water looked like any other ocean water. My friend knew that beneath the ordinary looking surface, there were hundreds of magnificent tropical fish and beautiful coral. As we swam together, we kept shouting, "Look at this one! Look at that one!" It was one of the most amazing days of my life. Physical vision opened a dimension of God's creation I had never seen or even imagined. Without a face mask, it is impossible to see underwater. I had often laughed at people who wore those stupid-looking masks and breathed through the snorkels. Before, without a mask, I was the one who was blind. I could open my eyes underwater, but could see nothing. With the face mask and a way to breathe, a magnificent new world awaited discovery.

3. With no vision, we cannot really see Jesus Christ. We may see church buildings. We may participate in church organizations and serve on church committees. We may read books about Jesus. We suffer from blindness to the central person. The leper *saw* Jesus, ran to his feet, and said, "Lord, if you choose, you can make me

clean" (Luke 5:12). If we do not see Jesus in compassionate ministry, in suffering upon the Cross, or in resurrection victory, our relationship to God tends to be based upon custom, tradition, or moralisms—never on anything truly transforming.

One pastor remembered an occasion of a particularly powerful vision: I was going through a difficult time in my ministry. I was discouraged. Feelings of failure haunted me. I prayed with a friend. As we prayed together, I inwardly saw Jesus approaching me with a bucket of water. The vision was so vivid that it was as though I were actually seeing and talking with a physical being. As Jesus approached me, he took the bucket of water, threw it over me, embraced me, put his mouth to mine, blew, and filled my lungs. The experience was so powerful that I told no one about it for years. I was not sure of the meaning of the vision. Gradually, I understood what had happened. It was a fresh experience of the grace of God in Jesus Christ. I had been washed anew and had received the new breath of the Spirit. I came into a closer relationship with God than I had ever known. I have never forgotten the vision. To me, it is a picture of the ultimate reality of God's amazing grace in action.

4. With no vision, we are blind to human need. Around us are the "walking wounded" whom we conveniently ignore. Comedian Dick Gregory tells a serious story about a time when, as a young man, he had been working all day. At the end of the day, he went into a small restaurant and ordered a cheeseburger, fries, and a milkshake. A shabby, disheveled man came in, sat on the stool beside him, and ordered a double cheeseburger, fries, and coffee. He shoved the food into his mouth as if he were starving. Moments later, he told the owner that he had no money. The owner took a Pepsi bottle and hit the man across the face, knocking him to the floor. Then he came around from behind the counter and began to kick the poor man viciously. Blood came streaming from his face.

Gregory watched in shock and horror. Finally, he jumped down from his stool and said, "Mister, don't kick him anymore! I'll pay for it!"

The man got up slowly, wiped the blood from his face, turned to him, and said, "Son, you don't have to pay for it; I just paid for it down there." He paused, then said, "But, son, if you were going to pay for it, why didn't you do it sooner? Why did you wait until it was too late?"

Visionless congregations are not deliberately cool. They just don't see!

5. Visionless congregations tend to see the church as a problem and

most members as apathetic, disgruntled dead weight. Visionless congregations almost always suffer from a crisis of low self-esteem. They are convinced they are too small, too poor, too weak, and too poorly located. This negative image tends to be contagious; it repels people with genuine need who are seeking help from God and/or people who could be enlisted as partners in ministry to help those desperately in need. Any of these persons who could be enlisted in ministry in the community simply do not have the time or energy to deal with a negative, depressing, fighting congregation.

B. RECOGNIZE CHARACTERISTICS OF CHURCHES WITH VISION.

1. A church with vision that is consistently affirmed and lifted up will always be an exciting, dynamic, energizing center of hope. Such congregations are not only effective as channels for the healing grace of God, but their ministry also helps prevent all sorts of human and social problems by their faithfulness to the gospel.

2. Visionary congregations tend to be responsive to human need, not only within the membership, but within the larger community. Congregations inspired by dreams and visions are usually involved in one or more major mission projects. These congregations tend to be Great Commission-centered, rather than self-centered. Their attitude tends to be, "We cannot do it all, but we can do something. What we can do, we will do, by the grace of God."

3. Visionary congregations experience the life of faith as an inspiring journey, rather than as a depressing obligation. There is a joyful contagion about these congregations. This posture of forward-leaning receptivity positions people to receive new visions that call forth new approaches to previously unseen needs.

Visionary congregations consistently enlist significant numbers of persons in some form of committed Bible study. The most exciting new approach to Bible study is entitled DISCIPLE: Becoming Disciples Through Bible Study.

DISCIPLE began as a shared vision in March 1986. Eighteen church leaders (including Bishop Richard Wilke) gathered in Flower Mount, Texas and committed to a dream of developing a pastor-directed Bible study for training Christian disciples. DISCIPLE aims at far more than the communication of information. To date, over 8,500 people have been trained to teach the Bible, and approximately 93,000 people have been involved in the study. The transformation of lives, congregations, communities, and the world is clearly seen as a long-range result of group Bible study, discussion, and prayer.

DISCIPLE anticipates disciplined participation. Each participant is to read the Bible thirty to forty minutes a day according to a carefully developed plan. Participants read about 75 percent of the Bible during the nine-month DISCIPLE schedule. Students read the Bible to hear the Word of God for their present-day lives. The use of a study manual helps students record insights and directions received.

One of the most exciting components of DISCIPLE is the use of ten-minute videotape segments for each of the thirty-four weekly study sessions. Video teachers are nationally known theologians, scholars, pastors, and church leaders.

Also unique to DISCIPLE is the youth component for 17-, 18-, and 19-year-olds. Often six to ten youth make up a DISCIPLE group. Slightly abbreviated assignments address the unique life situations of youth.

One of the most exciting unanticipated results of DISCIPLE has been the transformation of participating congregations. Through DISCIPLE, members identify their spiritual gifts and offer themselves in ministries of teaching, visitation, mission volunteering, and working with children and youth. Almost without exception the stewardship commitment of the church is deepened. Congregational unity and enhanced self-esteem of leaders result in a stronger positive impact of the church upon the community. Stories of lives transformed from Bible study are reported by hundreds of the DISCIPLE congregations. DISCIPLE is now being used in Korea, and will soon be translated into German and Spanish.

The demand for a follow-up to DISCIPLE has resulted in the preparation of DISCIPLE II: Into the Word—Into the World. The DISCIPLE Bible study story is truly one of the most dynamic accounts of vision-power in our time.

Another very effective study is the Bethel Bible Study. Launched by a Lutheran pastor in Wisconsin, Bethel is now widely used by numbers of non-Lutheran congregations. In the fifty states, six thousand one hundred twenty-eight churches are enrolled. About 85,000 teachers have been trained and are teaching or have taught more than 1 million participants. The Bethel approach uses pictures to help students grasp the content and meaning of the books of the Bible. The pictures actually serve as "vision carriers" to the meaning of scripture. Kerygma Bible Study and the Trinity Bible Study series are widely used in mainline denominations. Kerygma Bible Study approaches scripture around the great themes of the Christian faith.

39

For congregations involved in Vision 2000, we recommend a fifty-day commitment to daily Bible reading from Easter to Pentecost on the great vision of scripture. Congregations are urged to enlist persons for thirty minutes of daily scripture reading. Suggested readings are listed in Appendix B of this manual for such a study/reflection process (page 95). Vision 2000 congregations are expected to have Bible reading as a major emphasis as they approach ministry in the year 2000 and beyond.

As mentioned in "Steps to Take at This Time," p. 32, we suggest that Pentecost Sunday each year be designated as a day of receptivity for God's dreams and visions in each local congregation. Plan a Pentecost breakfast, and invite all new members received during the past year to be present. Invite them to share briefly what Christ and the church have meant in their lives. On Pentecost afternoon or evening, have a "dreams, visions, and possibilities" time with the whole congregation where all are invited to share their new and deepening visions for ministry. Be sure to have the Vision 2000 Team present in order to help discern where new visions need to be added to the existing list, and where existing visions need to be deepened with the help of new people. The purpose of this annual Pentecost event is to acknowledge and to celebrate the continuing openness of the congregation to new and deeper visions for ministry and to give thanks for God's continuing faithfulness in leading the people. (A supplemental resource dealing with vision sharing is *Growth Plus: The Vision* manual, pages 28-29, also published by Discipleship Resources.)

4. Visionary congregations welcome the presence of the Holy Spirit in the life of the church. These dynamic congregations recognize the dangers of "charisphobia" and "charismania." By "charisphobia," we mean an unbiblical, unwarranted fear of the gifts of the Holy Spirit in the life of the church. This may be present because of unfounded fears that the gifts of the Spirit will divide the church or will have a negative effect upon certain persons. Some charisphobia is the result of abrasive relationships between persons who identify themselves as "charismatic" Christians and those who might call themselves "traditional" Christians.

By "charismania," we mean an unbalanced focus upon the more unusual gifts of the Spirit (tongues, interpretation, healing, miracles) and a blindness to the central role of "agape" love (1 Corinthians 13). At times there has been a subtle elitism that tempts members to label, categorize, or classify each other. Such labeling is always divisive and hurtful. Paul has an important word for all Christians when he writes to the troubled church at Corinth. All believers are to find their "style" in Christlike love. All Christians are to understand that the Spirit is not given for personal status, but to continue the ministry of Christ through the church. Paul writes, "So with yourselves; since you are eager for spiritual gifts, strive to excel in them for building up the church" (1 Corinthians 14:12).

5. Vision-receptive congregations understand the implications of biblical teachings that relate the presence of the Spirit to prayer. Luke quotes Jesus as saying, "If you then, who are evil, know how to give good gifts to your children, how much more will the heavenly Father give the Holy Spirit to those who ask him!" (Luke 11:13). Contrast this with Matthew 7:11, which reads "good things" instead of "the Holy Spirit." Luke's focus upon the work of the Spirit in continuing the ministry of Jesus through the church is important to vision-receptive persons. These congregations are not at all surprised to learn that God's Spirit is joyfully and dynamically active in leading and empowering the church today!

Visionary congregations see the church in a new way. All the members are seen as children of God, gifted with one or more spiritual gifts for ministry, to continue the work of Christ in the world today! Apostolic hope sees church members in a positive way.

> From now on, therefore, we regard no one from a human point of view; even though we once knew Christ from a human point of view, we know him no longer in that way. So if anyone is in Christ, there is a new creation: everything old has passed away; see, everything has become new! (2 Corinthians 5:16-17).

6. Vision-receptive congregations are not strangers to portions of the New Testament that refer to spiritual gifts. These congregations understand that the spiritual gifts listed in 1 Corinthians 12, Ephesians 4, and Romans 12 are but samples of the gracious and amazing gifts God purposed to give for ministry through the church. Such congregations are genuinely excited about the potential of lay ministry and have one or more approaches to the discovery of spiritual gifts. Self-esteem is lifted in these congregations, not by manipulative praise, but by celebration of the goodness and faithfulness of God. The church celebrates not what it is doing for itself within the walls of the church, but what God is doing in the community and the world through the church. These congregations understand that each person is a valued member of the Body of Christ.

See the church in a new way. Develop a hopeful view of the church. Congregations that are attentive to biblical teaching inevitably see the church in a more hopeful and positive way. The church is not viewed as a denominational franchise or a stepping stone for pastors on their way up the ladder. The church is seen as more than a building, organization, or religious service club. The church is perceived as the front line of God's vision and purpose to bring all of creation together and to end the separation of persons from each other and from God.

7. The church is not seen as defeated and dying, but as moving and aggressive in its fight to defeat the destructive powers and structures. Jesus' statement to Peter takes on added significance in these enthusiastic congregations: "I will build my church, and the gates of Hades will not prevail against it" (Matthew 16:18). The vision here is the image of the church as a power that storms the very gates of ultimate opposition to God—and wins! The church is on the offensive, and the church breaks open the gates of hell to set the captives free.

The church becomes receptive to new vision for future ministry when it leans forward in obedient confidence that God's cause will not fail. The vision of overcoming replaces the picture of being overcome. Confidence replaces timidity as the church begins to image itself in a new way. It lives by exciting faith to communicate the possibility of faith. The church has to believe it will grow, attract new people, and be appealing. Then as it dares to live faith as if this were already happening, there is a miracle! God honors such faith, and the church becomes what it is meant to be.

8. Such congregations begin to handle problems and failures in a new way. Failure is not perceived as a disaster, but as a signal to regroup and to develop a new strategy or alternative approach. Fear of failure intimidates congregations into bland repetition of yesterday's programs. If a church's ministry experiences no failures, it probably signifies that very few creative visions have been accepted and tried. In *Thriving on Chaos*, Tom Peters writes, "There is an almost irreducible number of failures associated with launching anything new. For Heaven's sake, hurry up and get them over with!" Dave Boyer, president of Telefex, maker of high-tech control systems, talks about "failing forward." Learn from failure, and take the next and smarter step quickly.[9]

Most dynamic congregations can point to a long list of failures— ministries that just did not succeed. For example, maybe your congregation has tried an alternate worship service with times and styles that simply did not meet congregational needs. Maybe you have seen new groups or classes that have folded, or celebrations that turned out to be terrible disasters. The point is not that the congregation had failures. Instead of being defeated by the failures, however, they learned to laugh at them.

9. Visionary congregations keep trying new ideas. Vision is blocked by refusal to risk change. New visions are not given to those who kill visions they receive. As in the parable of the talents, visions buried in fear are lost. Only visions that are lived change lives and prepare for the wonder of continuous *vision flow.*

Become a vision-receptive congregation with effective ministry in and beyond the year 2000. Congregations receptive to Vision 2000 are encouraged now to assume the posture of leaning forward by using the process for congregational involvement outlined in this *Vision 2000* manual.

10. Visionary congregations are constantly sensitive to sections of the community that tend to be ignored. Many congregations have inadequate ministry to men. Contact your denominational men's club for information about the evangelism and mission program that they are sponsoring. Let a group of men come together to help reach other men and youth in organizations such as Scouting and athletic teams. All congregations would be strengthened by an emphasis upon the quality of Christian education and the quality of youth and children's ministries.

Remember—because you cannot do everything does not mean you cannot do something. Do what you can. Look for neglected areas of ministry: search for persons not involved in ministry; carry visions; communicate enthusiam; enlist additional persons in ministry for Christ in the church.

Begin now to pray for, to expect, and to experience vision-responsive ministry!

FOR REFLECTION, DISCUSSION, AND REACTION

1. Is there a need for a Vision 2000 experience in our congregation? Why?

    What are the needs?

2. Have you had an experience that enabled you to "see" things differently? Would you share it?

3. Is our congregation characterized by excitement? Energy? Enthusiasm? If so, where is it found?

4. Is "charisphobia" or "charismania" a problem in our congregation? How can members be helped to handle this problem?

5. Does our congregation "celebrate" what it is doing in the community and in the world? Illustrate how this can be improved.

6. When failures have occurred, have other or better ways been found? Illustrate.

VI | THE VISION CONTEXT

No vision can emerge from your experience or from your congregation apart from the context in which your life and that of your congregation is cast. This context is a vital part of what emerges. You remember the story of the child who, when reprimanded for his bad conduct, asked, "Dad, do you think it is heredity or environment that causes me to do these things?"

In a sense, we have both hereditary and environmental influences at work in the visionary process. They must not be allowed to control the process, however. In some instances they must be countered with a full understanding and appreciation of the importance of visual anticipation.

A. YOUR VISIONS ARE OF PRIME IMPORTANCE DESPITE THE NEGATIVE AND POSITIVE INFLUENCES THAT WILL BE WORKING ON YOU AND YOUR VISION 2000 TEAM.

1. Tom Peters, author of *Search for Excellence* and *Passion for Excellence*, quotes Father Theodore Hersburg, former president of Notre Dame University, who states unequivocally: "The very essence of leadership is that you have to have a vision. It has got to be a vision you can articulate clearly and forcefully on every occasion. You can't blow an uncertain trumpet."[10] Peters then tells of the vision of Steve Jobs, at the Apple Computer Center, who wanted to start a revolution in the way the average person processes information and deals with his or her world. And he did! Likewise, Fred Smith, the founder of Federal Express, envisioned a more reliable mail service and made it happen.

Literature on the subject of leadership invariably deals with the priority of vision. Leaders must be people who have a clear picture of the potential of the organization in which they are working.

2. Information can create mental pictures, or visions, which profoundly affect the way we work and what our expectations are. Robert Rosenthal's work at Columbia University is widely heralded as providing convincing proof of this statement. He has demonstrated the almost unbelievable impact of this dimension of vision.

In a classroom experiment (described in *The Pygmalion Effect—The Self-Fulfilling Prophecy*, McGraw-Hill Films) Rosenthal chose pupils who were identified to their teachers as unusually bright, "high achievers with a very high IQ." The children were, in fact, selected by random choice. They were the same as all others. At the end of the year, the children were tested. Those identified and envisioned as having high IQs and being unusually bright actually made higher scores and were judged by their teachers as more receptive, more eager, and more rapid learners.

Rosenthal's comment on this noteworthy experiment was that because the children were randomly selected, the variable existed only in the teacher's thinking. He then noted how teachers, having created their vision or image of a child, actually resented the high achievement of those who were not identified as bright or superior students. Like most of us, they didn't like to be wrong.

This same type of experience was repeated in a welding class in a vocational school. Certain members of the class were again selected by random and designated as HAPS (High Aptitude Performers). At the end of the term, it was evident that those selected and designated as HAPS had actually learned faster and were more proficient than others. The instructor was stunned when he was told about the experiment. He was convinced that he had treated everyone the same way. His vision of the different levels of possibility had unconsciously had a powerful influence upon the students' learning speed and performance.

Keep in mind as you proceed with your visioning process that your visions will be translated as "pictures of possibilities." The intensity with which you see them and the strength of your conviction that they are what God wants to have happen will have profound effects in their becoming the visions of your church and its leadership.

3. Don't let some casual comment, or even some strongly directed argument, keep you from believing in and knowing what you can achieve. All of us can be robbed of our best performance by losing our vision and doubting ourselves.

When most congregations are suffering from a poor self-image and a feeling of unexamined inferiority, they do not need to hear more negative judgments about their failures and inadequacies. At this point, they need affirmation and encouragement!

B. THE VISION CONTEXT AS SEEN IN THE RESTRUCTURING OF AMERICAN LIFESTYLES.
  1. Changes are taking place in our society. The United Way of America's Strategic Institute has "recently identified more than 100 specific trends in society and grouped them into nine major change-

drivers for the 1990s." They are called "Nine Forces Reshaping America" in *Futurist* magazine, July 1990. They are:

- maturation of America
- the mosaic society
- a redefinition of individual and societal roles
- the information-based economy
- globalization
- personal and environmental health
- economic restructuring
- family and home redefined
- rebirth of social activism[11]

All of these may be of some interest to you and your Vision 2000 Team, but some will have particular interest. One such "force" is "the maturation of America." Did you know that

- every day, on average, more than 5,000 persons are celebrating their 65th birthday?
- there are now more than 32,000 persons who are 100 years or older?
- men now celebrating their 65th birthday can expect to live 14.4 years and such women can expect to live 18.8 more years?
- at the age of 65, there are now 149 women for every 100 men?
- in the last 100 years, life expectancy has been increased by 28 years?

These statistics show that we are living through a demographic and cultural revolution, which necessitates new social activities, institutions, and programs. This also is the first time when so many have lived so long, when older adults have made up such a large proportion of the total population, when so many have lived alone, and when so many have so much to offer in their retirement to help others.

How will your envisioning include them? One large mainline denomination has stated that it will seek "to provide meaningful opportunities for senior adults to be responsive to the claims of God upon their lives and upon the world . . . to empower them for mission and ministry . . . to help them use their gifts, graces, experience, and skills and to share in the transmission of our faith heritage."

2. Another "force" that needs recognition in the local church is "the mosaic society." In years past, America was thought of as a "melting pot" where people of vast differences became blended into one. Today we are moving away from the mass society concept. Alvin Toffler, author of *Future Shock*, refers to this as "demassification." Each component of our culture has its own important place in the total mosaic.

This understanding can and should have particular relevance for churches serving areas where there is a significant diversity in the population. For example, churches that share a neighborhood with minorities such as Asians, African-Americans, and Hispanics will have unique opportunities and responsibilities. There are many stories of outstanding successes where established churches have envisioned and acted upon their visions to help organize fellowships, Sunday schools, and even churches for ethnic groups and served them through the use of their facilities.

3. The "force" of "globalization" at work in our future should produce powerful and positive results in the church's emphasis upon its missions ministries. Through satellite transmission of all that is happening throughout the world, we are more conscious today of the need to become "one world" than we ever have been. Continuing suspicion and hostilities around the world testify to the necessity of finding a willingness for all to seek and to develop the "common good."

4. Two other "forces" that are reshaping America, which may have special interest for your church, are "family and home redefined" and "rebirth of social activism." These forces need to be studied by proper groups within the church. These concerns need to be developed in your congregation. Your church may find new converts, new enthusiasm, and new opportunities for service by not only observing that the pendulum is swinging decisively in the direction of social concerns, but by acting upon it.

C. THE VISION CONTEXT AS SEEN IN THE WIDESPREAD INFLUENCE OF THE NEW AGE MOVEMENT.

Many members of mainline denominations are unfamiliar with the rapid growth of New Age literature and teachings, but it is a phenomenon not to be ignored. Recently it has been reported through the *American Bookseller* magazine that 2,500 bookstores now specialize in New Age books, 25,000 titles are now in print, and sales amounting to $1 million were up 30 percent over the previous year.

The New Age craze has created a market for all sorts of new products. In *Understanding the New Age*, Richard Chandler writes: "For a mere $99.95 you can buy a computer software program called Astrotalk. It provides your own personal astrologer with daily forecasts, accurate horoscopes, and other features. Just phone your order to 1-800-PLANETS."[12]

One might see a bit of humor in all of this. A sign in a New Age bookstore reads, "Shoplifting wrecks hell with your karma!" Far more serious is the fact that thousands of persons regularly pay from $10 to

$300 for "channeled" messages from the dead received through various spirit guides. Reincarnation is taken for granted in most of these circles as is the concept of the deification of the self.

On the positive side, however, there are areas of focus which Christians should be the first to consider. The areas include: (1) the strong emphasis upon the reality of non-material dimensions of existence; (2) the importance of protecting creation and the urgency of ecology issues; (3) the importance of the promotion of peace and world understanding; (4) the importance of holistic health, which includes proper diet, exercise, attitude, and self-image; (5) the call for radical change of mind and attitude for entering the future; and (6) the possibility of networking communities and individuals for greater effectiveness and mutual enrichment.[13]

D. THE VISION CONTEXT SEEN THROUGH THE GALLUP POLL STUDIES.

Another very important aspect of your vision context is your understanding of the American people about the church, their beliefs, and the practice of their faith. It will be extremely helpful for the Vision 2000 Team to share information that is available through George Gallup's recent study of America's faith in the 1990s. The poll provides an indication of receptivity about which we need to know. Statistics show that

- Nine out of ten Americans say they never doubted the existence of God.
- Eight out of ten say they believe they will be called before God on judgment day to answer for their sins.
- Eight out of ten believe that God still works miracles.
- Seven out of ten believe in life after death.
- One American in three claims to have had a powerful religious experience.
- Fifty-six percent of unchurched Americans say that religion is important in their lives.
- The primary reason the unchurched had not joined in the community of faith was that they had not been invited to do so.[14]

Gallup also reports that while religion is popular in the United States, it is largely superficial. Many lives have simply not been changed to the degree that would be expected from the figures given above. Gallup believes that we have become more critical of the churches and synagogues over the past decade. A large majority of those polled believe that churches are too concerned with internal organizational issues and not sufficiently concerned with spiritual matters. Many believe the church isn't concerned enough about social justice issues.

CONCLUSION

These facts are only a part of the "context" in which your church is now operating and will continue to operate through the last decade of this millennium and into the next.

Believe that new chapters are being written daily in the life of the kingdom and that your church has a vital chapter to write. Seize the opportunity now before you. Make your plans now for a breathtaking and spiritually renewing experience in your congregation, in your community, and in your world!

FOR REFLECTION, DISCUSSION, AND REACTION

1. Why are visions considered of prime importance?

2. Discuss your impressions of the Rosenthal experiment and how this may apply to your congregation.

3. Are you familiar with the New Age movement? Describe what you understand about it.

4. Turn to the Gallup study. What impresses you most?

What does this say to our church?

5. What would a vision for a decade of responsible ministry and
   evangelism in our church include?

What part(s) of this vision is (are) being done now in our church?

What part(s) needs to be added?

3 | STEPS TO TAKE AT THIS TIME

Yͦou are now ready to share the two most important sessions you will have. It is imperative that you and the Team be fully prepared. Success of the study is dependent upon making the proper preparations and taking each of the steps listed below:

1. Have you determined to take two sessions for Chapter 7?

2. Be prepared for the goal-setting process by doing the following:

A. Decide if you will use newsprint sheets or an overhead projector for listing the dreams and visions. Each Team member will need paper to prepare his or her "dreams" in the most succinct form possible. The lists of dreams will be turned in to the "secretary."

B. Take time to read aloud each item under 7-C, "Develop the Process for Envisioning," before beginning to list "dreams." This will enable each member to know how you are proceeding.

C. Name a person to provide all the equipment and supplies needed for recording the dreams and visions.

D. For the "measurable goals" found in section 7-D, you will need the following:

- Have one set of goal-setting cards prepared in advance for each member of the Team to use; a set will be comprised of one card for each of the eleven goals to be measured (see Appendix A, page 92).

  Number 1—Average worship attendance
  Number 2—Average Sunday school attendance
  Number 3—Professions of faith
  Number 4—New tithers
  Number 5—Persons going into full-time Christian service
  Number 6—New local ministries to be begun
  Number 7—Number of new congregations helped
  Number 8—Number of new overseas ministries
  Number 9—New ministries to be staffed
  Number 10—Changes in physical facilities
  Number 11—Social issues to be addressed

- Arrange for the cards to be color-coded by category if possible. This makes compiling the results easier.

3. Arrange to have a calculator at these sessions, for a quick summary of the totals and the averages.

4. Name one person to take responsibility for auditing the results of the Team's work, following the computation of each of the goals. This will verify the results before they are published or referred to others.

5. The compiled results should not be released in advance of the report to the governing body. Ask all Team members to cooperate completely whatever decision is made.

A note regarding the pastor's role:

The pastor has a critically important role to play in this effort. This is the time to demonstrate the biblical posture of "leaning forward." The pastor must persist in her/his vision quest until there is a clear picture of what the pastor believes to be the will of God in that situation.

This vision must be communicated in multiple ways to the congregation. If the pastor's vision is lacking, the local church vision for Vision 2000 will be greatly handicapped. Genuine enthusiasm, vibrant excitement, a confident sense of expectancy about the power of a vision will communicate the life-transforming potential of such a vision to the people. The entire process will be energized. It will be made contagiously exciting.

The pastor does not impose his/her vision on the committee, but rather maintains a delicate balance of holding to a vision while being flexible enough to allow the vision to be expanded, modified, clarified by lay input. This process of vision clarity and flexibility is expected at multiple levels of the Vision 2000 process.

The Vision 2000 Team also must seek clear visions and remain open to the congregation as new insights emerge. This emphasizes the importance of the process of annual Vision 2000 "dreams and visions" times during the year and particularly at Pentecost. Strong leadership by the pastor is essential for reclaiming Pentecost and celebrating the tremendous importance of every aspect of Vision 2000.

VII | DEVELOPING AND EXPERIENCING THE VISION

A. THE SETTING AND THE PROCESS.

You are now reaching the first milestone of your long climb to become a Vision 2000 church. Are you excited? Eager? Anxious? Good! You believe God is a vision-inspiring God. You have seen where scriptures and history demonstrate this. Now, believe that you too can enter into this experience that has the possibility of transforming your life, your family's life, and the life of your congregation.

1. *Don't delay!* Don't skip ahead to read the remaining chapters, promising to come back and do the envisioning at a more convenient time. Anticipate the importance of this effort and provide adequate time for it. Capitalize on this moment of opportunity. Remember Lord Chesterfield's oft-quoted advice. "Know the true value of time; snatch, seize and enjoy every moment of it. . . . Never put off till tomorrow what you can do today." This has special relevance when it is God's work which is to be done.

2. *Don't doubt!* Don't ask, "Who am *I* to be having dreams and visions for my congregation?" Believe that if Jesus could take twelve disciples and through them turn the world upside down with his message of love and truth, he can surely use what you and I have to offer. It is Jesus' work and will that we are seeking to know and to do. We are confident we will have the leadership and guidance of his Holy Spirit! Could it be that God is, even now, out ahead of us calling us to "lean forward"?

3. *Don't get hung up on numbers.* You may experience some resistance in establishing numerical goals to be reached by the year 2000. Leaders and team members should help each other to understand that numbers represent people, and *people* matter supremely! Numbers are reported in the Book of Acts on the day of Pentecost, on the day following Pentecost, and on other occasions. Numbers provided a way to celebrate the reality of God's mighty acts. Numbers will provide you with some measure of the seriousness of your congregation's response to Jesus' call.

4. You are not committed in advance to doing any of the things that will be suggested as visions. *Visions will begin to surface,* and these will bring other new ideas, which in turn will bring other new ideas. You will determine which suggestions you follow by evaluating these

visions in terms of the scriptures, traditions, experience, and current needs.

5. *Refresh your understanding* of the way the vision comes described in Chapter 5. Vision comes to congregations that are open to the Holy Spirit, to the gifts of the Spirit, to human need, and to new ideas. Raphael, the painter, claimed vision was the secret of his artistry: "I just dream dreams and see visions, then I paint around these dreams and visions." Seek the commitment of each member of your Vision 2000 Team to give all the time necessary to *faithfully fulfill the potential of this effort.* It cannot be rushed! It cannot be manipulated! It cannot be fully controlled by any member of the Team! Through prayer it can and will become a unifying, solidifying, awe-inspiring experience.

B. POSITIVE ANTICIPATION OF REALISTIC GOALS.

Jesus said to Nicodemus, as he described the work of the Holy Spirit, "The wind blows where it chooses, and you hear the sound of it, but you do not know where it comes from or where it goes. So it is with everyone who is born of the Spirit" (John 3:8). You will not be able to tell where these visions come from, how they arrived at this particular time, what they may mean in the life of your church, or even which visions are the ones that God is calling you to accomplish first. A divine transforming power is at work in this entire process, and it will be manifested and validated as time passes.

1. Begin this experience by focusing your devotional thought on the concept of "being co-laborers with Christ" in the work of his kingdom. Determine up front that all that is to be envisioned, suggested, and evaluated must center in the principles that Jesus exemplified in his life and in his teachings. There are too many important and basic expressions of loving God with all of your heart, mind, soul, and strength, and loving your neighbor as yourself to get caught up in or sidetracked by unimportant details.

2. You may find your mind drawing a blank the first time you seek to "dream dreams" or "see visions." Don't be discouraged! There are many ways to prime the pump for "envisioning." Many of the greatest dreams or visions have come as the result of needs being experienced—needs that gripped the mind, flooded the heart, and motivated the will. Those dreams or visions came with astonishing clarity; it was as though God asked, "Are you concerned? Can you do anything about this?" and you unhesitatingly responded, "Certainly." You didn't know at that moment how you might do whatever was required, but you knew a way could be found. So, you began to dream dreams of solving the problem, meeting the need, fulfilling

your desire to be of help, and doing what you believed God wanted you to do. This is envisioning.

3. We're aware of so many needs, and they are so varied, so involved, and so involving! How can we decide which ones we can address best? How can we know? As you begin to determine what to do, you may wish to remember Abraham Maslow's description of the hierarchy of human needs. He has suggested that all humans have the same basic needs, which can be diagramed in the form of a pyramid.

At the base of the pyramid are the basic "physiological" needs, which include food, shelter, clothing, and air to breathe—the basics necessary for life. At the next level is "safety"—our desire for security, stability, freedom from fear, structure, and order. "Belongingness and love" are third-level needs. These include desires for love, belonging, affection, friendship, roots, acceptance, peer approval, and loyalty. The fourth level, "esteem," emphasizes the need for strength, adequacy, achievement, confidence, independence, freedom, desire for reputation, respect, esteem, dignity. The fifth or top level is "self-actualization," the achieving of one's highest potential. We firmly believe that this is found only in losing one's life for the sake of others. Our self-actualization, as Christians, is made possible only through God's gift of atonement offered in Christ.

4. When you must choose one need to address, give thoughtful and prayerful consideration to which need strikes the greatest response on the part of the members, which need is most immediate in your neighborhood, and which need your membership is particularly adept in meeting.

C. DEVELOPING THE PROCESS OF ENVISIONING.

This process may vary with factors such as the number of members on your Vision 2000 Team; the accommodations of the facility in which you are meeting; and the availability of newsprint, blackboards, overhead projector, and tablets. Use whichever is best suited for your situation to give each member the fullest opportunity to express him/herself, to provide a full record of the suggestions for discussion, and to keep as complete a set of minutes as possible.

1. Before beginning, establish guidelines such as the following. These will in turn assure fullest participation:

   a. No negative comments will be made about any dream, vision, or suggestion offered. All will be received cordially without any negative reference such as, "We tried that one," or "We have never done anything like that."

   b. There will be no reference to the financial cost, the length of time it might take, the personnel that might be required, whether it might be unpopular or any similar negative observation.

c. Each participant will be given enough time both to list the dream and to explain it sufficiently so that the records can recall it in some detail.

d. If one suggestion inspires another of a similar nature, the two persons making the suggestions will have opportunity to say whether these may be considered together or should be kept separate.

e. You may wish to establish categories for the dreams or visions at the beginning, or you may wish later to identify the category into which they would fall. Either way, stimulate the thinking of the Vision 2000 Team so that all categories can be included.

f. Continue listing—without detailed discussion—until all possibilities have been enumerated. *This may require additional sessions.* Do not hesitate to adjust the schedule to provide for such.

2. Questions need to be addressed, such as: "What is our church's major task, our major purpose, our major responsibility?" "What other groups are seeking to relate to these needs?" "What expertise and what peculiar gifts do we have to utilize, which others may not have?" "Can we work cooperatively rather than competitively with other groups in this endeavor?"

3. Begin now the process of "envisioning" or "dreaming your dreams," asking God to show you what it is that God most wants you and your church to do in the immediate future, by the year 1995, by the year 2000, and into the next century. After your Vision 2000 Team has had ample time to list its visions, read the following section and formulate a worthy response.

NOTE: Depending on the amount of time needed to complete your list of dreams and visions, this may be a good place to divide the total work of Session 7 into two parts. If you have already needed more than one meeting to complete the list of "dreams and visions," don't worry. Take the time you need. The next part of your work in this session, designating "measurable goals," is a natural outgrowth of your dreams and visions. You will, however, move to a new and very important level of concreteness.

D. MEASURABLE GOALS RELATED TO YOUR CHURCH'S FUTURE.

In envisioning what the future could bring, it must be recognized that the primary and determining factor is "faith" or "belief." Remember again the words of Jesus to the man who asked to have his sight restored: "Do you believe that I am able to do this?" When Jesus had received an affirmative answer, he replied, "According to your faith be it done unto you." The scripture tells that the blind man's eyes were opened. He believed. He received.

We now want you to consider some measurable goals that will demonstrate what God can do in your congregation when you truly believe God's purposes can be accomplished. These goals are not lifted as ends in themselves. Rather they will come as by-products of the types of ministries you will develop, the spirit and environment you will create, and the intensity with which you will demonstrate your willingness to make disciples.

The naming of these goals is not a finish line or a tape at the end of the road, concluding the vision experience. Such goals must be thought of as journeys from the present, through all the stages which are to be developed, to arrival. During this process you will experience various stages of accomplishment. You will first envision, then perfect your vision, then communicate your vision, then overcome the credibility gaps, and, most important, ensure the participation of key leaders and members of your church in the vision. These persons must be willing to live regularly with and to experience these *kairos* visions through *chronos* time, improving them as they unfold.

1. AVERAGE ATTENDANCE GOAL BY THE YEAR 2000.
Worship is the most accurate barometer you have for determining the spiritual climate and forecasting the future health of your church's membership. Lyle Schaller and other authorities on church growth suggest that worship attendance is the most realistic evaluation of spiritual health.

What has been the trend in your church's worship attendance for the last five years, ten years, twenty years? This can be pictured on a graph. When did the trend begin, what caused it to develop, and what changes have taken place? What will the average worship attendance be in the year 2000 if this trend continues?

You have already conducted the Envisioning Sunday experience as a time to let the membership of your congregation join in choosing this goal. Your congregation looked at the pattern of attendance in past years. After a time of prayer and meditation, the members of the congregation registered their visions on the "Attendance Goal" cards. Now, as a team, it is time to lean into the future with the other members of your congregation. (It may be helpful here to have a summary of the earlier results available to each member of the Vision 2000 Team.)

Now envision your beautifully decorated sanctuary filled with people, joyfully expressing their praise and thanksgiving, sharing in the great hymns and music of the church, prayerfully lifting one another in intercession as supplications are offered for the needs of the world, and expectantly hearing the scriptures read and the Word proclaimed. Can you see it? Can you feel it? Is this God's will and purpose?

Let each member of the Vision Team prayerfully envision what she or he believes the average worship attendance can be by the year 2000 and write this number down on the appropriate card. The chair then asks the members to hold up their cards simultaneously for all to consider. Reflect on the numbers presented and then boldly record the most inspiring number upon which you *as a Team* can agree.

2. AVERAGE SUNDAY SCHOOL ATTENDANCE BY THE YEAR 2000.

Mainline Protestantism's "flight into blight" is said by some to have begun in the 1960s when the Sunday school was reorganized, considered less important, and given less support. Today the long-term health of the church is known to be in direct proportion to the vigor, vitality, and growth of the Sunday school. Bible studies have begun to assume their greatest importance in decades. People have a greater desire to participate in adult studies than has been true for years.

Now envision children, youth, and adults eagerly making their way into their carefully prepared and beautifully kept Sunday school classes, enjoying the warmth and comradeship, willingly accepting routine responsibilities to reach out and to greet visitors and prospects, and thoughtfully and prayerfully sharing the disciplined study of the lesson materials. Can you see it?

Now think of the worship attendance goal you have just established. Should your Sunday school attendance be a greater percentage increase than your worship service attendance? Let the Team members prayerfully envision what they believe the Sunday school average attendance can be by the year 2000 and write this number down on the appropriate card. The chair again asks members to hold their cards up for all to consider. Reflect on the numbers presented, and then boldly record the most inspiring number upon which you can agree.

3. NUMBER TO BE RECEIVED ON PROFESSION OF FAITH BY THE YEAR 2000.

Bishop Earl G. Hunt in his book, *I Have Believed*, states unequivocally, "To know the joy of belonging to God is to wish someone else to know it. To have Christ is to desire to share him with others. . . . The church is the only institution on earth which exists primarily for the sake of those who are not yet in it."[15] Faith sharing has now come into vogue in some of the mainline churches. Studies are available which teach how this is done in normal, nonthreatening, friendly relationships.

Envision key members of your church who have been so transformed by their experience of Christ, their love of the kingdom, and their desire to bring newcomers into the kingdom through your church, that they form a "caring, sharing, redemptive fellowship." Their basic commitment is to fulfill the command of Jesus to make disciples and they are willing to go and share. Experiences from growing churches validate the fact that new members win new members and often involve them in such a continuing ministry.

Prayerfully envision how many persons your church can reach and receive on a profession of faith between now and the year 2000 with this kind of experience at work. Again, hold your cards up simultaneously for all to consider. Reflect on the numbers presented, and then boldly record the most inspiring number upon which you can agree.

4. NUMBER OF NEW TITHERS TO BE ESTABLISHED IN THE CHURCH BY THE YEAR 2000.

There is no doubt from a reading of the parables of Jesus that he saw stewardship as a key issue of true discipleship. What we are doing with our lives, our gifts, our property, our time, our environment, and our planet inevitably determines the character of our Christian commitment. We have so much to learn and so far to go in achieving this form of true discipleship. Yet, we need to begin and to learn the truth—"to live is to give."

Tithing, the biblical practice commended by Jesus, is an overt way of establishing one's basic commitment. As pastors, we authors have never heard any tithers say they were sorry they had tithed or would never do it again. One year a local pastor became so enthusiastic about the benefits of tithing that he blurted out, "If you are not satisfied with the results of tithing in your own life, we will give you your money back." Two hundred families committed themselves compared to the ten families the year before. They proved the words of Malachi: "Bring the full tithe into the storehouse, so that there may be food in my house, and thus put me to the test, says the Lord of hosts; see if I will not open the windows of heaven for you and pour down for you an overflowing blessing" (3:10). This congregation was blessed and in turn became a blessing.

Now envision your church leadership and membership seeking to be faithful to the call of Christ to "come, take up your cross, and follow me"; to be faithful to those caught in the devastating circumstances of poverty, hunger, homelessness, illness, and despair; and to be faithful to their profession to uphold their church by their gifts. See them joyously extending their hands with their tithes, which will encircle the world in their ministry.

Now, prayerfully envision the number of tithers who will be a part of this congregation's financial program by the year 2000, and write this number down on a card. The chairperson asks the members to hold up their cards. Reflect on the numbers presented and then boldly record the most inspiring number upon which you can agree.

5. NUMBER OF YOUNG PEOPLE TO ENTER FULL-TIME CHRISTIAN SERVICE BY THE YEAR 2000.

A recently published report says that in 1966 the Roman Catholic Church had one priest for every 780 parishioners; today it has one priest for every 1,100 parishioners. If these trends continue, there will be one priest for every 2,200 parishioners by the year 2005. Fewer and fewer men are finding the priesthood attractive, and some of those already ordained are resigning.

In The United Methodist Church the number of pastors with annual conference membership is 39,719. Nearly 16,000 of these, however, are not related to the local church because of retirement, special appointments, or other reasons. The true ratio is one pastor for 395 members. The projection is that 40 percent of these present active pastors will retire before the year 2000. Comparable figures exist in most mainline Protestant denominations.

If the church is to turn the tide in membership in the immediate future, we must have the most personally attractive, educationally prepared, deeply spiritual, and authentically called youth our churches can provide. Can you envision the "cream of the crop" of your youth sharing such spiritual mountaintop experiences of Christ in your youth programs and congregational life that they will hear the call to full-time Christian service as pastors; diaconals in Christian education, music, missions, church program, finance, counseling, etc.; and others in specialized services.

Prayerfully envision your goal for new full-time Christian service commitments within your membership by the year 2000, and write this down on a card. Simultaneously hold your cards up for all to consider. Reflect on the numbers presented, then boldly record the most inspiring number.

6. NEW LOCAL MINISTRIES BEGUN.

"Just as you did it to one of the least of these who are members of my family, you did it to me," Jesus said as he described the last judgment

(Matthew 25:40). In the modern vernacular, service to others is where "the rubber hits the road." In our ministries we demonstrate whether our profession of loving our neighbor as ourselves can be justified.

In the first part of Session 7, you had opportunity to list your dreams and visions. No doubt your list included many new local ministries. Now select those ministry dreams that fall into this category, reflect on them, determine which have the greatest appeal among the team members present, and list them as goals for new ministries to be begun by the year 2000. Prayerfully hold these up for God's blessings, and write them down in bold letters.

7. NUMBER OF NEW CONGREGATIONS HELPED.

"New congregational development is happening across mainline denominations in many different areas and in many different ways," says James Cowell, pastor of Sandy United Methodist Church, Sandy, Utah. Places such as Tucson have developed what they call "a low capital intensive" plan by which they have organized four congregations within the last year. Partnership congregations are of primary importance. In the Missouri East Conference, two districts have challenged their congregations to "adopt a baby congregation" and underwrite its development costs.

Is this something that strikes a responsive chord in your thinking? Was your congregation helped in its earliest period by other congregations? Do you believe God is calling you to help extend the kingdom in this way? Could your congregation become interested in establishing an outpost Sunday school? Does a storefront ministry in a low-income area have merit?

If you are part of a small membership congregation, you can still be involved in encouraging a new congregation. Write a letter of encourage-ment; send a delegation to visit and greet the new congregation; offer the service of a choir or musical group from your congregation; receive a special offering to meet a pressing need in the new congregation; encourage members to purchase hymnals for the new congregation; or organize work parties for the new congregation site twice a year.

Prayerfully envision the number of opportunities you will create for assisting congregations and/or Sunday schools that may be formed or that are struggling for survival. Write these down on your card, hold the cards up for all to consider, and then record in bold letters the number of the congregations your Vision 2000 Team wishes to include.

8. NUMBER OF NEW OVERSEAS MINISTRIES TO BE BEGUN BY THE YEAR 2000.

In numerous consultations conducted by the authors, members were given "I Wish" lists to complete and return. These indicated things the laity were most interested in seeing done in the church and its ministries. Time and time again, the reports come back stating, "I wish we could have more mission teams of both youth and adults doing short-term missions projects."

In an earlier chapter we described the experience of one congregation with the Masai. What a transformation in a local congregation! Many other congregations have found new interest and vitality through sharing mission opportunities and working with people of other cultures. Is this something that God is lifting for you to consider? Do Jesus' words, "Go and make disciples of *all nations*" (Matthew 28:19) and "you will be my witnesses in Jerusalem, in all Judea, and Samaria, *and to the ends of the earth*" (Acts 1:8), strike a responsive chord?

You may wish to secure a list of "Advance Specials"—special mission projects—that are available around the world. This list may be obtained from your conference office. Try to select a project involving a person with whom your group can be in direct contact. The question becomes, "How many new overseas missions will you seek to begin before the year 2000?"

Short-term overseas volunteers in mission are serving in a powerful way in most mainline denominations. Contact your state or district headquarters for information regarding short-term overseas oppor-tunities. You may know of doctors, dentists, teachers, or pastors who have served as short-term overseas volunteers. Ask several members of your Vision 2000 group to telephone or speak personally with these volunteers. Report this feedback to the Vision group and in a newsletter article to your entire congregation.

Envision your congregation in direct contact and ministry with overseas congregations. (This can be Central or South America as well.) Antici-pate what it feels like to be so warmly received, so eagerly heard, so expectantly prayed for, and so amazingly empowered to do what may have seemed impossible. Project in your imagination what the results of this relationship may mean not only to those visited, but also to the visitors and to your congregation.

Now prayerfully envision your dream for the number of overseas ministries you wish to share in, either by personal visits or by financial support, and hold these numbers up for all to consider. Reflect on these, and then record in bold numerals the ones you choose.

9. DEVELOPMENT OF CHURCH STAFF.

In his book, *The Multiple Staff and the Larger Church*, Lyle Schaller asserts: "The majority of all congregations averaging more than 200 at worship on Sunday morning are staffed either to remain on a plateau or to decline in size. Only a small proportion are staffed for numerical growth."[16] Are you expecting to break the 200 barrier? Do you hope to make visible progress toward reaching it? Or are you now well beyond it? Whichever category you may be in now, you are dependent upon your church staff not only for the routine forms of ministry, but also for the vision, leadership, inspiration, motivation, training, and development of overall strategy. Here again, needs of your particular parish will indicate staff positions that must be filled.

Can you now envision able, dedicated, enthusiastic persons, lay and clerical, serving part-time or full-time, who have excellent training or who are willing to be trained for the particular staff positions you need? Can you picture the results of their ministries in the lives of children, youth, singles, young adults, older adults, persons with handicapping conditions, and the poor? Can you envision needs being met in such a magnificent way that scores and scores of people find their way to your congregation.

Now, prayerfully envision your dream for the particular ministries you believe should be staffed by the year 2000. List positions to be filled rather than the number of full-time staff persons to be added, and write them down on your card. Excellent ministries are now being developed by part-time staff members. Hold these cards up for all to prayerfully consider, and then record in bold letters the ones you choose.

10. CHANGES IN PHYSICAL FACILITIES.

Do your dreams for the future entail a change in the appearance of your buildings? Modified or enlarged buildings? New structures? A change in location? Before making quick statements about these needs, perhaps consideration should be given to the "image" that your present facilities present as well as the space they provide. A change of image may be a "basic" requirement if your church is to have a continuing opportunity in the future. Accessibility, both in its geographic location and its physical features, will determine future opportunities as much as the beauty of the buildings.

Facilities, by their design and appearance, should look as though something wonderful is happening here. They should communicate, "God is smiling on this spot, and we want you to be a part of all the exciting things that are happening inside."

If radical changes are necessary in your facilities, you may wish to dream dreams of "spaces" needed for the ministries that you dream can be fulfilled. Architects have the ability to wrap the functions and the forms of ministry that you hope to include in the outer shell of buildings.

If modification, beautification, and increase in the amount of space are all that is needed, you may find a real thrill in envisioning what could happen, how the modification would look, and how it could be utilized.

Now prayerfully envision the physical changes you believe are most necessary for your congregation to meet the challenge of the new millennium, and write these down on your cards. Describe these in broad outline. Paint this word picture with bold strokes until it can emerge from the imagination and be captured on the papers you are preparing. Hold cards up for all to consider, then write down your decisions boldly.

11. SOCIAL ISSUES TO BE ADDRESSED.

What are the social issues to be addressed by the church by the year 2000? Does the congregation have a tradition of being a "peace" church or of being committed to environmental concerns? Do the leaders know in what areas members are presently volunteering their time? Would that information be helpful? Ask members of your vision group to rate each of these issues using a scale of 1 to 10. (1 is of least concern to you; 10 is of greatest concern.)

a. _____ world peace
b. _____ the environment
c. _____ homelessness, hunger, and poverty in America
d. _____ drug and alcohol abuse
e. _____ medical problems—AIDS, Alzheimer's disease
f. _____ racial justice and harmony
g. _____ crime and violence
h. _____ others _____

_____

After discussing these social concerns and issues within your group, consider the advisability of involving the congregation in a sample concerns rating. Is it possible to identify several areas of concern for a two-year period of concern, education, and action—leading to and continuing beyond the year 2000?

FOR REFLECTION, DISCUSSION, AND REACTION
(AFTER THE "ENVISIONING" SESSION(S) IS/ARE COMPLETED)

1. What are the three "don'ts" that were avoided?

   Any problems here?

2. Did you draw a blank at first? What did you do?

3. What guidelines did you establish?

4. How many "visions" were listed?

   In how many categories?

5. Was a positive, enthusiastic, confident attitude generated before the measurable goals were enumerated?

Were you surprised by the results? In what way?

6. Was more time needed?

How many sessions have now been devoted to "envisioning"?

7. Did you use any feedback from the congregation? How?

8. Are your measurable goals properly recorded in minutes of the meetings?

4 | STEPS TO TAKE AT THIS TIME

You have now amassed a wealth of material, all under the heading of "Dreams and Visions." You have two sets of material. One set is the "measurable goals" that you developed for the eleven items listed on your goal cards. The other is the "dreams and visions" that were listed prior to the measurable goals. Some time will be needed for the Team to faithfully handle all that has been compiled. The following guidelines may be helpful:

1. FIRST, A WORD OF CAUTION NEEDS TO BE STATED. The vision has come. The vision must now be shared. Those who commissioned the Vision 2000 Team in the first place—the governing body and the congregation—wait for a report and for the opportunity to take hold of the vision. The Vision 2000 Team must not allow itself to become viewed or to view itself as a body charged with the task of completing the vision—deciding what is and is not to be done—or bringing the vision to reality. The major contributions this study and this Team can make are to *inspire*, to *stimulate*, to *motivate*, and, by example, to *encourage* others to boldly take up the dreams and visions and make them their own.

2. A FIRST STEP IS TO DETERMINE WHAT IS THE BEST WAY IN YOUR CONGREGATION TO PRESENT AND TO SHARE THE VISION, given the structure of the governing body and the various forms of ministry already in place. What is the best course of action to follow? Will you:

    a. Simply file your report with the governing body of the congregation and surrender it? We hope not.

    b. Plan a "retreat" or other special vision-sharing event to make a full presentation to the governing body, and eventually to the congregation? Such an approach will give you maximum opportunity to invite and to share ownership of your results in a way that best supports the vision you have received.

3. ASSUMING THAT YOU WILL PLAN FOR SOME KIND OF VISION 2000 SHARING EVENT, we suggest that the following steps be taken:

    a. Plan a "Vision Alive" retreat.

b. For this initial vision-sharing experience, invite only the governing body of the congregation and the Vision 2000 Team to be present.

c. Designate and recognize those who attend this event as the "Vision Alive Group"—a now expanded group (larger than the Team by itself) who will be responsible for carrying the vision to the congregation.

d. Plan your Vision Alive retreat with two major purposes in mind. First, you want to focus on the "measurable goals," *to celebrate* the vision that has been received. Second, you will work with the list of "dreams and visions," *to begin planning* together for the best way to share the vision with the rest of the congregation. Let's look at each of these major objectives for the Vision Alive retreat.

4. THE FIRST PURPOSE IS TO CELEBRATE THE VISION THAT HAS BEEN RECEIVED. The focus should be on the "measurable goals." This should be an occasion for the governing body to *recognize* that the Vision 2000 Team, which was duly commissioned, has now reached a milestone. The journey is not over. In fact, the Vision Alive Group as a whole—Team and governing body—may feel a bit breathless. But this is not a time for questioning or debating the goals. Dreams have been dreamed. Visions have been received. This is a time for celebration. Discussion of how to achieve specific goals and which goals should have priority will follow. For right now, be sure as a governing body and as a Team, *as the Vision Alive Group,* to share this moment of ownership. God has been faithful thus far. God will be faithful as you lean into the future together. Several things can help you achieve this celebration.

a. Because the Vision Alive retreat is for sharing the vision, the event should be co-sponsored by the Vision 2000 Team and the governing body.

b. Ask the pastor or key lay leader of the governing body to be in charge of the celebration and to introduce the meeting by recalling the highlights of what has happened since the Team was first commissioned.

c. Then call upon the Team to present the report of its measurable goals. You may want the Team chairperson to present these. Or you might ask various members of the Team to present various goals in keeping with their own interests and enthusiasms. In any event, this should be seen as a time of reporting and celebrating, and the report should be as concise, as clear, and as inspiring as possible.

d. After the report of measurable goals has been given, the pastor/

leader of the celebration should guide the group in receiving the report.

1. Remind the Group that this is not a time to question the figures, but to celebrate them and what they stand for—a positive movement in this congregation to lean forward into the future with bold faith and hope.

2. Also, this is the time to recognize those goals that will become official. In order to be recognized as a Vision 2000 Congregation by the Section on Evangelism of the General Board of Discipleship, the goals for *average attendance* will have to be approved by the governing body as stated goals for the entire congregation. Having heard and received the report of measurable goals, the Vision Alive Group may want to approve other goals in this way as well.

e. A good way to close the celebration would be to have a brief time of worship together. Give thanks to God for the visions that have been received. Ask God for strength and wisdom to understand, to plan, and to introduce the vision into the life of your congregation as it approaches the next millennium.

5. THE SECOND PURPOSE OF THE VISION ALIVE RETREAT IS TO BEGIN PLANNING THE BEST WAY TO INTRODUCE THE VISION TO THE REST OF THE CONGREGATION. Once an appropriate celebration of the measurable goals has taken place, the Vision Alive Group can move to this second step of sharing, planning, and owning the vision. For this step, you will begin working in more detail with the list of "dreams and visions" generated in Session 7.

a. Let the Team chairperson be in charge of this process.

b. Place the list of dreams and visions, including any preliminary categories into which they have been analyzed, before the entire Group.

c. Have some members of the Team prepared to give a brief interpretation of the list and any preliminary categories.

d. Invite the whole Group—Team and governing body—to review this list, to discuss any preliminary categories, and to suggest other ways in which the list might be better divided and organized. (Note: Vision 2000 Team members must be especially careful at this point *not* to feel that they must defend their initial ideas about organizing the list. Remember, this is a time to share wisdom and ownership.)

e. Continue working together by relating each of the categories of ministry, or each of the visions, to a general "timeline." Which are "immediate," "short-term," "medium-range," or "long-range" dreams and visions?

f. Discuss which of these have the greatest interest and support in the congregation. Ask each member of the Group to rate the dreams on a scale of 1 to 4 as follows:

> 4 . . . very important
> 3 . . . important
> 2 . . . as time permits
> 1 . . . unimportant

Remember, in tallying the results for each dream, the largest number indicates the highest priority.

g. Analyze the dreams, visions, and categories that receive higher priority, and discuss recommendations for presenting these to other appropriate individuals or groups in the congregation who have related concerns. Capitalize on the momentum that has been created. Find ways to let some of the dreams and visions develop among interested persons with the creation of as little structure as possible. (Many excellent ideas have emerged and become realities in a short period of time when those interested are "unleashed" and given the opportunity to "do their thing" for the kingdom!)

h. Invite members of the Vision Alive Group to personally present these findings to other groups and to the congregation as a whole. This will generate the kind of enthusiasm that the Group members have.

i. Plan as a Group to keep the Vision 2000 theme before the congregation. Each of the following will help you achieve this:
- Use the church bulletin, newspaper, announcement sheets, etc., to publicize the continuing work of the Vision 2000 Team.
- Announce the formally adopted goals for average attendance (and any other formally adopted goals) to the congregation.
- Continue to follow up on the actions that are being taken. Let every group that is involved in any of the dreams and visions know that reports are welcomed by the Vision 2000 Team.
- Have the Team begin planning now for the next Pentecost celebration of new and deepening visions.

6. BRING YOUR VISION ALIVE RETREAT TO A BRACING CONCLUSION BY HAVING A SECOND TIME OF WORSHIP TOGETHER. Include an opportunity for individuals to share what the retreat event has meant to them and what they think the vision can now mean for the rest of the congregation. Spend a time of covenant together, recognizing that the way ahead will not always be easy, but giving thanks to God's continuing faithfulness as you lean forward with bold faith into the future together.

VIII | KEEPING THE VISION ALIVE

A. DEALING WITH THREATS TO VISION.

Members of the Vision 2000 Group should not take it personally if they experience some resistance to the visions and goals they present. When a congregation deals seriously with launching new ministries in the local community, expanding the base of tithers, and encouraging new congregations as well as beginning new overseas missions, there will be some apprehension. When significant goals are set for worship attendance, Sunday school attendance, and additions on profession of faith, some anxiety will arise in the community of faith.

Identifying social issues to be addressed by the year 2000 is in itself an assignment guaranteed to lift all sorts of differences of opinion. Still, the issue is too important to be ignored. The thought of starting new classes and groups and of having new people coming into the church when new ministries are launched will lead many people to conclude there is a possibility of a significant change in their beloved local congregation. Change is always disturbing. As strange as it may seem, it seems less frightening for a congregation to continue its decline and the inevitable journey toward futility and death.

Realize that although some people will grumble and perhaps a few will drop out, many others will be attracted by what the church is doing and will be excited about the new possibilities for ministry. People outside the walls of the church will become excited by the Vision 2000 focus of ministry. Still it is helpful to identify in advance some common vision threats. Along with the identification of some of these vision threats, we shall propose strategies for dealing with these potential problems.

B. RELATING TO THOSE WHO HAVE NO VISION.

Some people in each congregation will find the whole discussion of vision to be virtually meaningless. Some people do not think visually. They are strictly left-side-of-the-brain thinkers—logical, sequential, analytical, and with virtually no visual or graphic capacities. Many of these persons are those who have been trained to work with their hands or to think mathematically. There are three steps for relating to persons who maintain they have no vision.

1. Realize the problem may be in the use of words. The word *vision* may carry negative or mysterious suggestions that practical people

avoid. Try more familiar words such as *long-range plan*, *the big picture*, *a different point of view*, or *plan for the journey*. Substitute the term *pictures from the manufacturer's handbook* for *visions from the Bible*. Don't let the vision vocabulary be a barrier to communication and inclusiveness.

2. Enlist the help of those who experience difficulty with vision in gathering statistics or making projections about the community. Maybe some members of your congregation are skilled statisticians or are adept at making future projections based on past data or interview samples.

3. Ask persons who express difficulty with vision formation or communication to explore other areas in which they may feel more at home. These persons may be able to do a superb job with demographics. Demographic studies provide valuable background for vision formation. Remember both left- and right-side-of-the-brain persons are needed. Visionaries and practical realists can create a great team. Persons who feel uncomfortable with vision vocabulary but who are skilled with the use of computers can create superb graphics to help the church understand past trends and future projections. Remember the balance in the biblical perspective between a *kairos* and a *chronos* awareness of time. Do not allow the use of the word *vision* to become a barrier or to create an elitist group. You will remember that God's grace is bigger than visions.

A number of references have been made regarding the importance of visions to Paul. He writes to the Corinthians, " . . . I will go on to visions and revelations of the Lord. I know a person in Christ who fourteen years ago was caught up to a third heaven—whether in the body or out of the body I do not know; God knows. And I know that such a person . . . was caught up into Paradise and heard things that are not to be told. . . . Therefore, to keep me from being too elated, a thorn was given me in the flesh . . . " (2 Corinthians 12:1-4, 7).

According to Paul it is possible to become "too elated" or too visionary or too spiritual in an esoteric sense. Some bothersome physical ailment, which had to be endured, came to him. Paul says that he prayed about the problem. Instead of the removal of the difficulty, he was given the word, "My grace is sufficient for you, for power is made perfect in weakness" (2 Corinthians 12:9). At the center of it all, Paul said in effect, it is not in thrilling visions or exciting spiritual ecstasy that God's greatest gifts come. The real wonder is the wonder of God's unfailing grace, which meets us in the day-to-day challenges of life. Paul added, "So, I will boast all the more gladly of my weaknesses, so that the power of Christ may dwell in me . . . for wherever I am weak, then I am strong" (2 Corinthians 12:9-10). According to Paul, the apostolic posture is not "too elated" by vision but in living in gratitude for God's amazing grace in Jesus Christ. That is the *kairos/chronos* posture of a Vision 2000 congregation.

C. KEEPING THE VISION ALIVE.

Vision 2000 congregations will want to take three steps to keep the vision alive. With each step an effort must be made to look *to and beyond* the year 2000 and to relate the developing vision to existing structures within the congregation. Because this manual is written as an ecumenical resource, it seems inappropriate to suggest how to relate the vision and dream to any one particular denominational structure or policy. Therefore, we offer the following suggestions:

1. Allow short-term task groups of interested and motivated persons to begin work immediately on one or two of the visions that arise from the Vision Alive retreat. The best time for the formation of these task groups is often right after the dreams and visions have been received and a small nucleus of concerned persons has been identified.

Opportunity for participation in ministry areas or projects can be publicized in the bulletin or newsletter. Announcements should be made concerning the formation of a new ministry (task) group to address a particular issue (e.g., hunger, homelessness, etc.). Everyone in the congregation who is interested in this area of ministry should be invited to meet at a particular time to develop action plans.

If existing work areas or committees are already functioning, they should be encouraged to join with the newly forming group. These task or ministry groups are free to enlist additional help from the congregation. "Turf battles" are avoided by a strategy of mission that sees all structure as releasing persons for mission rather than keeping and controlling mission responsibilities for certain people or groups. In other words, the overarching objective is to deliver help to people beyond the church rather than to worry about getting everything neatly into existing committee structure. The strategy is to unleash the church for Christ's work in the world rather than to maintain an organization.

2. Invite the help of your district, synodical, or presbytery officer to plan with you ways of using existing congregational structures and systems to further the vision. Key leaders of a congregation should be involved with the pastor and denominational executives in this

process without becoming blocked by any groups or individuals who are creating resistance to vision.

In terms of seeking a consultant beyond the membership of the congregation, you might also consider inviting a visionary leader to visit your congregation as a Growth Plus Consultant. The Growth Plus process is very similar to the one outlined in this book. Highly motivated and experienced Growth Plus consultants are available in every section of the country to visit your congregation and to assist you in vision formation. These consultants are able to serve in a variety of denominations because the Growth Plus process is authentically nondemoninational. For additional information order *Growth Plus: The Vision* manual (order no. DR052 from Discipleship Resources, toll-free 800-685-4370 or fax 404-442-5114). If you would like a consultant to visit your congregation, call the Growth Plus office at (615) 340-7052.

3. Look for other ways to connect your vision with leadership beyond your own congregation. Such leadership can help you:

a. Recognize existing and emerging strengths in ministry and build upon these.

b. Listen to congregational and community leaders in order to discover additional unmet needs. Visionary leaders will bring new ideas in meeting these needs.

c. Learn from other visionary congregations. Find a congregation with a slightly larger membership that is alive, growing, and engaged in levels of ministry. Take a team to visit this congregation on Sunday morning. Arrange to meet with pastors and some of the lay leaders on Sunday afternoon. Notice bulletin boards, materials, and resources. Discover ideas that can be used in your congregation. Remember that such "creative sharing" of ideas is great stewardship!

d. Plan to attend a seminar at a teaching church such as Frazer Memorial in Montgomery, AL; Whitefish Bay United Methodist Church in Whitefish Bay, WI; Ben Hill United Methodist Church in Atlanta, GA. For help in identifying components of churches of vision, see *Tried and True* and *Every Member in Ministry*, both by John Ed Mathison (see Suggested Resources, p. 101). Other vision resources include the book *Extending Your Congregation's Welcome* by W. James Cowell (Discipleship Resources, order no. DR068). An excellent newsletter called *Net Results* is available by calling toll-free 1-800-638-3463 or by writing Subscription Office, 5001 Avenue North, Lubbock, TX 79412-2917. Other teaching churches will be identified as part of Vision 2000 within the next five years.

Each summer before the vacation period begins, urge your members to visit dynamic, growing churches as they travel. Invite them to bring home ideas and sample resources. Contact the pastor in advance to arrange an interview with key leaders after the worship service. Ask the pastor and other leaders to share their vision; explain the process by which the vision was received; explain the plan they followed to keep the vision alive; and tell how they continue to integrate emerging visions with the ongoing life of the church.

These visits to parable churches can be particularly helpful to members of the Vision 2000 Team. Have members of the Team contact other congregations to interview pastors asking the same kinds of questions.

e. Share vision resources. Visionary leadership can help you become a vision sharing congregation yourself. Nothing encourages your own vision like seeing it inspire others.

Encourage your denominational leaders to allow time at conferences and gatherings of laity and pastors to share new vision resources and ideas. Instead of focusing primarily upon problems and difficulties, share one practical, helpful idea for ministry at every meeting! Don't be afraid to share some enthusiasm and excitement about new strengths, new learnings, new responses, and new materials that relate to Vision 2000. Remember, most of our best ideas have been learned from each other. Help create a more open atmosphere of sharing. Persist in communicating the vision.

FOR REFLECTION, DISCUSSION, AND REACTION

Answer on a separate sheet.

1. Have you experienced some resistance to your work either inside or outside the Team? How have you handled it?

2. Discuss the problem of change and how you plan to approach this problem in your congregation.

3. Have you dreamed dreams that will create doubt? Skepticism? How can this best be handled?

4. Have you reviewed the "STEPS TO TAKE AT THIS TIME—4"? Which of these do you need to follow more fully?

5. Is your church "unleashed"? Is it free to explore, develop, project, and minister where there are needs? If not, what can help it become "unleashed"?

6. What denominational leaders could you invite to work with you on problems of vision resistance?

7. What visionary congregations in your area can you visit in order to refresh your own vision?

IX | COUNTDOWN 2000

A. STEP INTO THE FUTURE.

Use your imagination with us again as we step forward into the future to focus upon seven specific, rapidly approaching dates. Recall the distinction between *kairos* and *chronos* time. We look at seven specific *chronos* dates that are filled with amazing *kairos* possibilities.

1. The *first Sunday of Advent 1999*. You are singing with the congregation the Advent hymn, "O Come, O Come, Emmanuel." As the refrain becomes more and more familiar with each verse, more and more people join in singing, "Rejoice! Rejoice!" and in asking Emmanuel to come. Worship attendance, which has been growing steadily in recent years, is higher than ever! This is the last Advent before the year 2000. Purple paraments and stoles are in place. An Advent candle is burning at the Advent wreath. People stand for the reading of the Gospel. The text is from Mark 13:32-37. Mark 13 is called the "little apocalypse."

With the growing excitement surrounding the dawning of the year 2000, and with the increased sale of books predicting that the year 2000 will mean the end of earth time, and with the end of time and the second return of Jesus Christ, people listen expectantly to the words, "But about that day or hour no one knows, neither the angels in heaven, nor the Son, but only the Father. Beware, keep alert; for you do not know when the time will come." . . . "Keep awake." . . . "Keep awake."

This message deals with the importance of both the first and the second advent of Jesus Christ. This word of hope and encouragement is given to people who have been saturated with so much apocalyptic media hype. The congregation is unusually receptive to questions of faith, ultimate meaning, and value. The congregation concludes the worship by singing, "Come thou long-expected Jesus, born to set thy people free."

Would it be appropriate on this first Sunday of Advent to invite persons who have never done so to receive Jesus Christ as the Lord and Savior of their lives? Do you plan to share together in Holy Communion on this Advent Sunday? You can relate this Eucharistic meal with the great messianic banquet! How does the biblical message contrast with the media hype?

2. Now it is *Christmas Eve 1999*. Multiple services of worship have been scheduled. Attendance is larger than on any other Sunday. The candlelight service has been announced in advance. Each worshiper holds a small candle. The Gospel reading, Luke 2:1-20, for Christmas Eve is heard: " . . . to you is born this day in the city of David a Savior, who is the Messiah, the Lord" (Luke 2:11). Worshipers at the 11:00 P.M. service may also hear the Christmas Day Gospel, John 1:1-14: "The light shines in the darkness, and the darkness did not overcome it" (John 1:5).

During the service each worshiper is invited to set a personal worship attendance goal for the year 2000. Three-by-five cards are distributed. Important personal commitments are made. Each card contains the person's name and address with a number representing the numerical goal for Sundays to be present in worship in the first year of the new century. Cards received at the time of the offering are dedicated at the altar. (These cards are to be mailed back before Pentecost Sunday with a letter of encouragement and appreciation for worship attendance, which has broken all previous records. The letter also offers a word of encouragement for continued faithfulness during the summer Sundays.)

The sanctuary is darkened except for the light of a single candle. The light is shared. Darkness is pushed back. The congregation stands to hold high the candle as all sing together "Silent Night." The year 2000 is rapidly approaching. Some persons will wish to remain after the congregation has left for a moment of silent prayer and meditation in the sanctuary.

3. It is *New Year's Eve 1999*. The service of worship has been well publicized, with invitations extended by the congregation throughout the community. An attitude of excitement and expectancy is obvious as the congregation gathers.

A thousand years ago St. Peter's church in Rome was packed with people who believed the year 1000 would certainly mean the literal return of Jesus Christ and the beginning of the last judgment. In the final year of 999, people gave away lands, homes, and household goods to assure for themselves forgiveness and a place in heaven. Many entered St. Peter's clothed in sackcloth, with ashes poured over their heads. The floor around the altar was covered with arms spread out in the shape of the cross. At the altar, Pope Sylvester II was celebrating the midnight mass. Richard Endroes writes of that moment in *Living on the Brink of Apocalypse*:

> When the fatal hour struck, the crowd remained transfixed barely daring to breath, not a few dying from fright, giving up the ghost then and there. The moment passed and the earth did not open to

swallow the church and worshipers and when no fire fell from heaven, all stirred as if awakening from a bad dream. Then amid much weeping and laughing, husband and wife, servant and master, embraced. Even unreconciled enemies held each other as friends and exchanged the kiss of peace, and the bells of every church on the seven hills of Rome began to ring as a single voice.[17]

What hymns will be selected for the final service of 1999 and for the first service of the year 2000? Use the lectionary readings: Old Testament, Ecclesiastes 3:1-13; Gospel, Matthew 25:31-46; and Epistle, Revelation 21:1-6a. What will happen at the hour of midnight in 1999? What worship experience will be planned for the long-awaited dawning of a new century?

4. The *first Sunday of 2000*. Announce in advance the beginning of the twenty-first century worship loyalty emphasis from January through Pentecost for the year 2000. Train members to invite friends and neighbors. Recall Gallup's data indicating that most persons are outside the church because they have not been invited by a credible witness. At this first service in January, set a tone of worship that is intentionally more vibrant and dynamic. Consider carefully the music that will be used the first Sunday of the year 2000. Music and worship style could help establish a new pattern that will enable the church to be more effective in its ministry. This will certainly be another very important moment in time—*kairos* and *chronos*—for the congregation. Worshipers hear the ecumenical lectionary in the Gospel reading from Mark 1:9-15. Hear the word of Jesus, "The time is fulfilled, and the kingdom of God has come near; repent, and believe in the good news" (Mark 1:15). Vision 2000 congregations will plan carefully to allow persons to respond to his call.

5. The *first Sunday of Lent* may be a time to encourage all persons to participate in a small sharing group during the Lenten season. Also encourage members to do something in ministry to meet an unmet need in the community. The Lenten season provides the *kairos* moment for teaching spiritual discipline and for commitment to acts of peace and justice.

6. *Easter 2000*. Imagine the first Easter of the year 2000. The congregation is singing together, "Christ the Lord Is Risen Today." Again the sanctuary is filled. There is an awesome note of receptivity. The congregation hears the words of the Easter Gospel from John 20:2-18. Some persons present will have the experience of recognition described in the text. Some will be able to say with Mary, "I have seen the Lord!" Will there be an opportunity on this first Easter in the year 2000 for response to such vision? On Easter Sunday every worshiper is

invited to join in fifty days of daily prayer and Bible reading on the theme of the kingdom of God and the work of the Spirit (see Appendix B, p. 95). Easter to Pentecost is a time of high motivation and commitment to share the resurrection, hope, and victory of Christ in the local and larger community. It is a time of invitation, visitation, and ministry focus. Daily prayer for a new openness to God's Spirit is encouraged from Easter to Pentecost. The congregation unites in daily silent prayer at 7:00 A.M. "O God, send your Holy Spirit to guide and empower us for the ministry of Christ in whose name we pray. Amen." Confirmation or training classes are held for youth and adults to be ready for public commitment and church membership on Pentecost Sunday.

7. *Pentecost 2000*. This is a great festival! Members of the congregation are encouraged to wear something red in recognition of the liturgical color of the day and to communicate the note of hope and festivity. The new-member breakfast honors all new members received since January. These new members are invited to share their personal witness about what God is doing in their lives. Pentecost worship for the year 2000 is dynamic! Contemporary Christian songs and hymns add to the new excitement for worship services.

Look at the Gospel in John 15 and the Pentecost message in Acts 2. The message announces that the celebration is not about what has happened but about what is still happening! It is about the celebration of the fact that the age of the Spirit is the authentic "new age."

The congregation returns in the afternoon to share in the annual dreams, visions, and possibilities experiences. Commitments are made on Pentecost Sunday to attend an eight-week leadership training course taught by pastor and laity for potential leaders. Through this seminar leaders are equipped to continue visionary service through the church to the local and larger community.

During the summer months pastor and congregational leaders attend what is the first prayer/Bible study and planning retreat of the year 2000. This retreat leads to deeper commitment to Jesus Christ; greater openness to the Spirit; and commitment to continue long-range visionary planning as a regular part of congregational life. From this posture, commitment, great faith, and joyous expectancy emerge. The church continues each year to respond to God's guidance for ministry and mission.

The church leans forward and continues to express its life through seven great vision areas: a) inspiring worship; b) dynamic Christian education; c) winning evangelism; d) transforming local ministries;

e) world outreach; f) faithful stewardship; and g) adequate staff and facility to enable Christ's ministry to be more effective.

Believe! This can be your vision for ministry by the year 2000 and into the next century!

X | PRACTICAL IDEAS FOR CONTINUING THE JOURNEY INTO THE 21ST CENTURY
(A PERSONAL WORD TO OUR READERS)

At this point you may be feeling overwhelmed by a flood of ideas and suggestions. We know from experience that such material can bring anxiety and guilt as well as insight and inspiration. Remember, you don't have to do everything at once. These are ideas for the years ahead. Also, you don't have to do everything alone. You can invite and train other leaders to share the work with you. As you read, continually remind yourself that you do not have to do everything yourself. Be aware that you can delegate to many people who are waiting to be asked.

There are practical ideas that you can begin to use now as you look to the year 2000. These ideas and concepts will be very important as you continue the momentum of your planning and ministry process. Vision 2000 recognizes that the journey has not ended when the date 2000 is reached. These ideas come from the pastoral experiences of your authors and from leaders of many denominations.

A. AFFIRM A GREAT PURPOSE.

Never forget, or allow members of the congregation to forget, that what you are doing as a church *really* matters! Your mission is important! To have such responsibility is an awesome privilege. The church is an outpost of the kingdom of God! It is a sign of the coming victory and reign of God over all of the universe. The church is the family called to continue the ministry of Jesus Christ in the power of the Spirit. We are the Body of Christ. We are his ambassadors—his witnesses. We have powerful marching orders: "Go into all the world." We are the carriers of the vision. The faithfulness of every person and every congregation really matters. Share the vision that comes from your Vision 2000 Group work. Communicate your purpose and your mission. Express enthusiasm for what you are about. Clear articulation of belief and passion for purpose will be essential.

B. CELEBRATE THE PRIORITY OF WORSHIP.

Focus constantly upon the fact that the center of the faith community is to be found in the worship and praise of God. Understand that worship is truly the ultimate *futuristic* activity. It is the one thing that we do on earth that scripture tells us we shall be doing beyond death. Celebrate the anticipatory character of the Lord's Supper. The meal is the sign of the great messianic banquet in which the power of sin and death is finally broken.

Recall the power of praise in worship. Utilize hymns and songs that move beyond words about God or Jesus Christ to words of praise and gratitude sung to God. Offer a variety of styles of worship and music when more than one service is offered on Sunday morning. Let the traditional hour remain largely unchanged. Make contact with those outside the church through the use of more contemporary Christian music. Variety in styles of worship within the same congregation will increase outreach. Let the service move—not drag. Let the preaching communicate passion. In the twenty-first century the basic principle of communication will still be true. Seven percent of our communication is verbal. Thirty-eight percent is by tone of voice and 55 percent is body language. Let the worship leaders communicate the good news in every way! Preaching in the twenty-first century will be increasingly biblical, narrative, and visual.

C. RECOGNIZE THE IMPORTANCE OF THE FRIENDSHIP FACTOR.

Gallup's study of the unchurched American indicates an increasing receptivity of persons outside the church to personal invitations to worship. In most congregations 83 percent of first-time visitors have been personally invited by friend, neighbor, or relative. Many of those outside the church say they would attend if invited—and they would in turn be willing to invite others! Train the congregation to constantly invite others. Churches that invite, grow. Churches that do not invite, decline.

Most persons eventually select a church not on the basis of denomination or pastor, but by their perception of being authentically valued and wanted within that particular church. Many persons in the twenty-first century will be looking for a supportive, caring family. Alvin Toffler, writing of any future organization that is relevant says, "It must restore community." With the expansion of the high-tech, low-touch society of the future, caring Christian touch—the contemporary equivalent of the ancient "kiss of peace" will be important. Greeter teams, section greeters, nametags, and immediate first-time visit follow-up will be vital tools. The mobility of the American people will increase. Today 20 percent of the population move annually. Fifty percent change denominations when they move. Outreach to the lonely must be recognized as a vital Christian ministry. The deep hunger for meaningful relationships will be recognized as a priority issue.

D. OPEN NEW PORTS OF ENTRY.

A "port of entry" is a doorway through which new persons can enter the church and through which existing members can return to active participation. Study the groups that are now "ports of entry" in your congregation. Organize new groups to meet recognized needs. Consider a group for parents of blended families, a group for parents of preschool children, and a group for recently retired adults. Choirs, exercise groups, and study groups can all become effective ports of entry with the training and encouragement of persons to warmly welcome and encourage every visitor.

E. RECOVER THE POWER OF PRAYER.

Encourage daily Bible reading and prayer. Use a daily devotional guide such as *The Upper Room*. Invite persons to come to the altar rail during the pastoral prayer or during a time of invitation. Encourage participation in "Cursillo" or the "Walk to Emmaus." For information concerning *The Upper Room*, Walk to Emmaus, and Cursillo, write to The Upper Room, P.O. Box 840, Nashville, TN 37202 or call (615) 340-7200. Lead healing services in which intercessory prayer, Holy Communion, and laying on of hands are vital elements.

F. BE OPEN TO THE SPIRIT.

Understand the reasons for charisphobia and charismania. Focus teaching on the Person and work of the Holy Spirit, with emphasis upon the fruit of the Spirit. Help each person to perceive herself/himself as "gifted" with something to share in ministry for God. See the congregation and the church in a new way—filled with gifted people who could be released to utilize their spiritual gifts.

G. EXPERIENCE THE POWER OF THE CHRISTIAN YEAR.

Allow the ecumenical lectionary (developed by the consultation on common texts) to provide structure for celebration of the great *kairos* moments in the ongoing *chronos* pattern of the Christian year. While maintaining the traditional core of each festival, think of new ways to make the meaning of the great festival days more vivid and exciting.

H. ENCOURAGE TEAM SPIRIT AMONG LEADERS.

In the twenty-first century, there will be an increasing awareness of the importance of team spirit among leaders of every area in the life of the church. Old-style, formal committee structures will be inadequate for people increasingly oriented toward ministry rather than meetings. The building of high trust levels and the valuing of the input from every person on the team will be increasingly important. An excellent resource for this purpose is Thomas Hawkins' *Building God's People*, available from Discipleship Resources, order No. LA070.

Team-building workshops will be essential for large-membership church staffs. Team teaching is "in" at every level. Team leaders for youth, children, adults, older adults, and singles ministries are the wave of the future. Volunteer teams will serve for specific projects at specific times in local congregations. Overnight work and planning retreats will be the order of the day for church leaders and officers. At such time, long-range planning (from five to ten years in advance) as well as annual planning is needed. Remember the team approach to new visions and dreams at the annual Pentecost "dreams and visions" workshop.

In every area of congregational life, small sharing groups should be encouraged. Every group that meets—from ushers to trustees to lay visitors—should be encouraged to begin and end with prayer. The formation of a friendship circle in which persons join hands is a good way to symbolize the team approach of the congregation to every area of ministry.

I. PLAN SOME NEW SPECIAL EVENT EACH YEAR.

Avoid the trap of repeating the same old programs each year. Look for possibilities of innovation. What could the congregation do that would be new and fun? What would help people play together? Celebrate together? Plan something new so that persons can experience the sheer joy of Christian life.

J. ENABLE LAY MINISTRY.

Each year, envision new ways of opening doors for lay ministry. Find new ways to "release" laity for ministry. One idea is having lay ministers of pastoral care who call on all members twice a year. A devotional guide written by the members of the church is distributed during Lent by these visitors. Late summer or early fall, each member receives a visit with a brochure describing the program of the church for the next twelve months.

K. BE AWARE OF THE NEEDS OF SPECIAL GROUPS.

Plan to meet the needs of a growing older adult community. Contact leaders of the Hispanic community and plan a crosscultural fiesta. Plan ministry for first-time mothers, singles, divorced persons, and bereaved persons. What can be done to encourage more participation of men? What about a father/daughter banquet or a father/son banquet?

L. REMAIN AWARE OF THE COMMUNITY NEEDS THAT NO ONE IS MEETING.

A church in Sri Lanka in the midst of a very poor community keeps several wedding dresses to loan to brides who cannot afford a wedding dress. The church also provides transportation from their community to the hospital. The church has a most unusual ministry. There is a shed behind the church where laity donate their time and effort to make coffins, because people of the community are so poor they cannot afford a coffin when someone dies. What could your church do to meet the needs of hurting persons who have been ignored in your community?

M. STRENGTHEN THE FINANCIAL BASE.

Plan annual dinners that celebrate the grace of God and the wonder of God's gifts to and through the congregation. Encourage tithing as an expression of gratitude and commitment.

N. ENCOURAGE PEOPLE TO SET GOALS.

Encourage worship goals, Christmas Eve and Lenten attendance goals, and giving and service commitment goals.

O. CONTINUE TO ENCOURAGE DREAMS, VISIONS, AND POSSIBILITIES.

Plan to keep the date on every Pentecost Sunday afternoon to open the door for new visions and new dreams. Understand that Christian existence is a journey of faithfulness to God who continually shares new dreams and visions.

P. REMEMBER THE IMPORTANCE OF SAYING "THANK YOU."

On Communion Sunday enclose a $4'' \times 6''$ affirmation card in the bulletin. Encourage every person to fill out an affirmation card to a church member or community person who is seldom recognized or thanked. These may be placed in the offering plate and mailed by the church. Develop the habit of saying "Thank you." If the church is large enough to do so, utilize a computer to generate a birthday letter to each member, which is mailed monthly.

Q. PLAN AN ANNUAL EVENT TO FOCUS ON EVANGELISM AND OUTREACH.

Plan a New Life Mission, a Key Event, a New World Mission, a preaching mission, or several days of special focus upon lifting up the priority of evangelism in the life of the church.

R. CELEBRATE VICTORIES; BUILD ON STRENGTHS; EXPECT GREAT THINGS FROM GOD!

Connect up with Abraham, Sarah, Isaac, Joshua, Moses, Ezekiel, Esther, Ruth, Jesus, Peter, Paul, and John; lean into the future with joyous certainty. Be open to the positive word of the gospel. Remember the word of Christ who says, "I am with you always, I will never fail you or forsake you." And Paul's affirmation, "I can do all things in Christ who strengthens me."

Understand that the church has to image itself in a new way. It has to live faith before it can communicate faith. By faith the church must believe the impossible. Your congregation has to believe it will grow and attract people. As a result, your congregation will begin to act as if those things were already happening. Then the vision begins to be realized!

CONCLUSION

Congratulations!

You have now completed weeks of study, reflection, discussion, praying, and envisioning. We pray that this has been an epochal experience for you and each member of your Vision 2000 congregation. We pray that when the year 2000 comes, many member of your congregation can look back, recall when Vision 2000 became a part of your church's planning, and give God thanks for the difference it has made in the life of your church. We pray that you will say, "It's miraculous! It is nothing less than a miracle," and that you will continue to believe in and have miracles happen.

We close as we began this journey, saying that vision is a gift of God but it is operative only as we use it. Harvard ophthalmologists report that our eyes have the greatest concentration of complexity of any organ in our body. Tens of millions of electrical connections handle over 1½ million messages simultaneously. Yes, simultaneously! Each one of us moves our eyes more than 100,000 times a day. If we exercised the muscles of our legs as much as our eye muscles, we would have to walk fifty miles a day.

But, it is only as we use our eyes, focus them, and receive these images through our lens onto the retina where millions and millions of receptors flash them to the brain at a speed of more than 300 miles an hour, that we can see. Yes, it is in making the effort that we see, but it is a miracle, nonetheless.

Now, think, if you will, how sometimes sight begins to dim and dimness steals across a person's eyes. Vision is fading, and blindness is approaching. Even now we can rejoice, for God has made it possible for people to go to an ophthalmologist and in a 30-minute surgical procedure have a diseased cataract removed so that sight is restored.

We want you to believe that this same kind of miracle can happen when we begin to lose our "spiritual vision," when we find ourselves losing our spiritual sensitivity, our awareness, and our ability to dream dreams and know that God is leading us. How marvelous it is to go to the "Great Physician" and experience the healing touch that restores our spiritual sight and gives us again the ability to "see" God's will and purpose. True, we may have to have more than one touch, as did the blind man who only saw "men as trees walking," but Jesus wants us to see perfectly, too.

NOW, ENVISION YOUR CHURCH AS HOPE-INSPIRED, HOPE-ENERGIZED, AND HOPE-REALIZED BY THE COMING OF THE YEAR 2000! Can you envision your church in the year 2000? Can you see it in a beautiful picture like this?

- Its buildings look as though they are saying with a smile, "Cleanliness is next to godliness" and "We worship in the beauty of holiness."
- Its members hurriedly stream into Sunday school and worship: Children, faces eager with excitement, run to the outstretched arms of their teachers; youth, laughing and joking, catch up on the latest news; adults, affectionately greeting each other, inquire about their mutual concerns; and strangers, immediately identified, are introduced and taken to warm and welcoming classes.
- Its worship service is regarded as a "mountaintop" experience for all who crowd into the sanctuary—with its spirited singing, its great choral music, its quiet moments for reflection and prayer when God seems closer than breathing, nearer than hands and feet; with the inspiration and revelation that come when God's Word is read and proclaimed; and with your sense of identity with the needs of the entire world as your offering is received and the plates, filled to overflowing, are lifted high before the altar as you sing "Praise God from whom all blessings flow. . . . "
- Its seven-day-a-week ministry, for all who will participate, encompasses every form of ministry for children, youth, and adults through group study, fellowship time, and service projects. Each ministry is designed to meet all types of physical, mental, spiritual, and emotional needs, which are found both within the local community and then around the world.

Can you envision such a picture for your congregation. Can you see it clearly? Are you in this picture? Will this picture become a reality? Will it grow brighter and brighter as the years of this decade pass and the new millennium comes?

Now, before you go, close your eyes after you read these words, and walk into this future. See it clearly! Let it be indelibly imprinted upon your mind. Feel what it is like to be a part of it. Experience it with every sensory nerve you possess!

Then, while you are still experiencing it, thank God for making it a reality—a reality now in your mind, and in the future a reality in your church! Amen and amen!

MATERIALS FOR THE ENVISIONING EXPERIENCE OF SESSION 5

1. *Vision 2000 card* to be filled out by the membership in worship, two Sundays before the Vision 2000 Team is to begin its study of Chapter 7.

VISION 2000—ATTENDANCE GOAL

As a member of this church, I am happy to "dream" with you about how many people I believe we can be serving by the year 2000.

I believe we can have _____ in worship each Sunday.

I believe we can have _____ in Sunday school each Sunday.

---

2. *Bulletin or church paper copy* to be used the week before the members will fill out their Vision 2000 attendance cards:

ENVISION YOUR CHURCH AS HOPE-INSPIRED, HOPE-ENERGIZED, AND HOPE-REALIZED BY THE COMING OF THE YEAR 2000!
Can you envision your church in the year 2000, can you see it in a beautiful picture like this:

See its buildings looking as though they are saying with a smile, "Cleanliness is next to godliness" and "We worship in the beauty of holiness."

See its members hurriedly streaming into Sunday school and worship: children, faces eager with excitement, running to the outstretched arms of their teachers; youth, laughing and joking, catching up on the latest news; adults, affectionately greeting each other, inquiring about mutual concerns; and strangers, immediately identified, being introduced, and taken to warm and welcoming classes.

See its worship service regarded as a "mountaintop" experience for all who crowd into the sanctuary—with its spirited singing, its great choral music, its quiet moments; with the inspiration and revelation that come when God's Word is read and proclaimed; with your sense of identity with the needs of the entire world as your offering is received and you sing "Praise God from whom all blessings flow. . . . "

See its seven-day-a-week ministry, for all who will participate, encompassing every form of ministry for children, youth, and adults through group study, fellowship time, and service projects designed to meet the physical, mental, spiritual, and emotional needs of our people.

You can envision such a picture for your church!

Will you come this Sunday and register your dream of what our average worship and Sunday school attendance can be by the year 2000?

3. *Membership and attendance record chart* to be compiled and carried in the church bulletin or paper the Sunday members are asked to "dream" of what their congregation can be by the year 2000.

Date	Membership	Worship	Sunday School
1970	_____	_____	_____
1975	_____	_____	_____
1980	_____	_____	_____
1981	_____	_____	_____
1982	_____	_____	_____
1983	_____	_____	_____
1984	_____	_____	_____
1985	_____	_____	_____
1986	_____	_____	_____
1987	_____	_____	_____
1988	_____	_____	_____
1989	_____	_____	_____
1990	_____	_____	_____

4. *Suggested pastor's prayer* to be used just before members are asked to sign their Vision 2000 cards, indicating their "dream" of what the church membership and attendance can be by the year 2000:

"O Lord, our Lord, how excellent is your name in all the earth. You have been our dwelling place in all generations. Before the mountains were brought forth, or even you had formed the earth and the world, even from everlasting to everlasting, you are God. A thousand years in your sight are like yesterday when it is past, and like a watch in the night.

"We come today rejoicing that you are our God and we are your people. You have called and we have answered. We rejoice that we are privileged to be a part of your church, the Body of Christ. Today, particularly, we rejoice that you are giving us an opportunity to "dream dreams," to have a "vision" of what this church can become by the year 2000 and into the new century.

"Open our eyes just now and enable us to see by faith that which can be, that which you desire this church to be. Give us the courage not only to register our vision, but to be faithful in helping this vision to become your reality. Our prayers we make in the name of your Son, our Savior, Jesus Christ. Amen."

Vision 2000 anthem available

A special anthem for Vision 2000 has been written by the Reverend Wes Putnam. The music follows the theme of the leaning forward of biblical persons named in Chapter II. "Vision" is the title of the song. It may be ordered by calling 1-800-733-5066. A demo tape is available from Wes Putnam, 214-418-8444, or from Tempo Music at the 800 number.

FIFTY GREAT DAYS— EASTER TO PENTECOST
SUGGESTED DAILY BIBLE READINGS
(Place in bulletin for Easter Sunday.)

Place this guide in your Bible for fifty days of Bible reading and prayer from Easter (the resurrection of Christ) until Pentecost (the giving of the Holy Spirit and the birthday of the church). Arise fifteen minutes earlier each day to allow time for this brief reading. Pray daily. "Thank you, God, for helping me be the person you want me to be. Enable our church to be faithful to you. In Jesus' name, Amen.

CHECK OFF AS YOU COMPLETE THE READING.

_____	1) God's call.	Isaiah 6:1-8
_____	2) Peace.	Isaiah 2:1-5
_____	3) The Messiah.	Isaiah 11:1-3
_____	4) A day of hope.	Isaiah 11:6-11
_____	5) Wings as eagles.	Isaiah 40:1-31
_____	6) Water in the desert.	Isaiah 41:17-20
_____	7) Getting through the rivers and fire.	Isaiah 43:1-17
_____	8) The vision of a new day.	Isaiah 43:18-25
_____	9) The promise of the Spirit.	Isaiah 44:1-8
_____	10) Peace like a river.	Isaiah 48:17-22
_____	11) God like a caring mother.	Isaiah 49:13-18
_____	12) Vision of the future.	Isaiah 51:11-16
_____	13) Vision of the suffering servant.	Isaiah 53
_____	14) Visions of resources for the journey.	Isaiah 55
_____	15) Vision of justice.	Isaiah 58
_____	16) Vision of light over darkness.	Isaiah 60
_____	17) Good news to the afflicted.	Isaiah 61
_____	18) News too good to keep.	Isaiah 62
_____	19) New creation.	Isaiah 65:17-25
_____	20) Result of sin and rebellion.	Jeremiah 4:23-31
_____	21) Tree planted by water.	Jeremiah 17:5-8
_____	22) Hope for your future.	Jeremiah 31
_____	23) Valley of dry bones.	Ezekiel 37:1-14
_____	24) River in the wilderness.	Ezekiel 47:1-12
_____	25) Love for rebellious child.	Hosea 11:1-9
_____	26) Outpouring of the Spirit.	Joel 2:28-29
_____	27) Vision of judgment.	Amos 8
_____	28) Vision of restoration.	Amos 9
_____	29) Victory of God.	Micah 4

_____ 30)	Deliverer from Bethlehem.	Micah 5:1-9
_____ 31)	Vision of king on a donkey.	Zechariah 9:9-12
_____ 32)	Tempting visions.	Luke 4:1-13
_____ 33)	Vision of Jesus.	Luke 4:14-30
_____ 34)	Vision of Jesus.	Luke 9
_____ 35)	Vision of Jesus.	Luke 10
_____ 36)	Vision of Jesus.	Luke 15
_____ 37)	Vision of Jesus.	Luke 19
_____ 38)	Vision of Stephen.	Acts 7:54-60
_____ 39)	Vision of Peter.	Acts 10
_____ 40)	Vision of Peter.	Acts 11
_____ 41)	Vision of Paul.	Acts 16:6-10
_____ 42)	Vision of Paul.	Acts 18:9-10; 26:19
_____ 43)	Vision of Paul.	Acts 27:23-24
_____ 44)	Vision of John.	Revelation 5:1-14
_____ 45)	Vision of John.	Revelation 7:9-11
_____ 46)	Vision of John.	Revelation 21:1-7
_____ 47)	Vision of John.	Revelation 22:1-5
_____ 48)	Vision for the day before Pentecost.	Acts 1
_____ 49)	Vision for the day of Pentecost.	Acts 2
_____ 50)	Vision for the day after Pentecost.	Acts 3

FOR ADDITIONAL READING

_____	The dream of Jacob.	Genesis 28
_____	The dream of Joseph.	Genesis 41
_____	Dreams and visions in the Book of Daniel.	
_____	Visions of Zechariah.	

MOBILIZATION OF AN ANNUAL CONFERENCE FOR VISION 2000

Vision 2000 looked like a gift from God to the design team for church growth in Western North Carolina in the spring of 1989. We had interviewed church growth leaders from across the nation and reviewed in detail several programs which were sufficiently comprehensive in scope to use across a judicatory just over 275,000 members in a mainline denomination. *Vision 2000* had both the flexibility and the marketability we were looking for. We were in a twenty-year pattern of consistent net membership losses while our state was gaining a steady 6 percent population a year. Our quadrennial priority was about to be adopted as a resolution of flourishing rhetoric—"the renewal and growth of every established church (1157 local churches), the organization of new congregations, and the redevelopment of certain congregations in crisis." *Vision 2000* gave the laity and clergy an image of leaning forward in faith and hope toward the 21st century. The Commission on Evangelism and Church Growth "fleshed out the vision" with a holistic, comprehensive program designed to help local churches grow again.

The *first* and fundamental step toward vision and growth is the *appointment of a diverse Vision 2000 Team* that includes someone new, someone "whose motions in the Board meetings always pass," someone single, someone who is not yet a full member, a young adult married person, and a chair who can get things done. *If the standing committee on evangelism is used to implement the following program, it will likely fail.* Why? Because at the first meeting someone will say, "Before we start getting new people in this church, I move we try to reactivate some of our members that used to come."

Secondly, mobilizing a judicatory that is mixed in maintenance mode attitudes and ministry requires a jolt! We borrowed a term from Herb Miller's writings and gave intensive promotion to the *Vision 2000 Launch Event* in mid-autumn. Our targeted audience were the local church Vision 2000 Teams and the pastors. For six hours on a Saturday the "fleshing of the Vision" Launch Event included music, messages, local church evangelism model seminars, and a drama entitled "Reaching the Baby Boomers." Over 2000 people came and Vision 2000 was put on the agenda of local churches!

The *Local Church Evangelism Models* were promoted as a cafeteria line from which each local church should choose the one model best suited to its needs. The entire local church Vision 2000 Team was invited to go to this seminar. After a two-hour introductory overview on the afternoon of the Launch Event, all-day seminars were led by the same faculty in early January, providing the local church teams with the "know-how" to go home and make that model work for an entire year. That was the plan! What happened was that the cafeteria line was so attractive that lots of churches spread out their team to cover several models! Faculty were proven leaders who had demonstrated their recommendations in local churches. Some were authors whose books were used as texts:

Extending Your Congregation's Welcome, taught by W. James Cowell, United Methodist General Board of Discipleship staff, using his book of the same title as a text. This is an introductory course to the principles of growth which orient a church to the needs of unchurched people rather than the customs of the churched!

Lay Visitation, taught by Stan Copeland of First UMC, Houston, using that church's manual entitled *Aldersgate Club* and supporting leaflets entitled "Four Calling Waves." The Aldersgate Club recruits members to proactively bring first-time visitors; the calling waves are follow-up groups.

Faith-Sharing, taught by George Morris of Candler School of Theology, using the book of the same title which he co-authored with Eddie Fox. This enunciates a United Methodist theology of evangelism and witnessing, followed by a section on methodology of relational evangelism that is person-centered, not institution-centered. Lack of self-confidence and denominational reticence have kept most United Methodists silent about a theology and a church that is holistically redemptive, abandoning the faith-sharing arena to fundamentalists.

Reaching Baby Boomers, taught by David Brazelton, Assistant General Secretary, Evangelism Section, General Board of Discipleship, reflecting his years of effective parish ministry and hundreds of local church consultations. Across the spectrum of the U.S. society 4 percent of the population are United Methodist, but only 1.1 percent of the Baby Boomer age group are United Methodist. Other mainline denominations show a parallel "drop-out rate" for this group. The people have almost no denominational loyalty. To reach them demands a pastor and a local church "paying the price" of meeting their needs.

Ministering with Singles, taught by Nell Mohney of Chattanooga, TN, using her manual "Singling Out Singles for Ministry." Fifty-three percent of today's adults in the U.S. are single; most churches are oriented to a married lifestyle. Mainline churches talk about meeting people where they are, but churches who are more rigid in theology are more flexible in program ministry.

Older Adult Evangelism, taught by Sam Seizart of Englewood UMC in Florida, helps local churches see retirement as a window of opportunity for the church. Retirement forces lifestyle change and often involves moving to a new community. Many people are open to going back to church for the first time since childhood—we know how and are willing to minister to them.

Mobilizing Volunteers for Ministry reflects John Ed Mathison's book *Every Member in Ministry* as he has practiced the celebration and equipping of the gifts of the laos. Most churches enhance, extend, or effect ministry with additional paid staff. This concept rediscovers the general ministry of all Christians.

Over 2500 laity were trained in one or more of these models. Hundreds of churches use all or some modification of the models and their respective implications for the life and work of their parish. Professions of faith in the WNC Conference increased in 1990 by 11.5 percent after declining 50 percent over the previous thirty years.

Worship Attendance Crusades in every church from Lent to Easter or Easter to Pentecost were emphasized through trained District Coordinators. Sixty-four percent of the local churches used this time to utilize "FRANgelism." Every member uses a form to list one Friend, one Relative, one Acquaintance, and one Neighbor who is functionally unchurched and covenants to *bring* them to church. Also, each church member signs a commitment card to attend church during the Sundays of the crusade. Participating churches gained 13 percent in attendance and 8 percent in membership.

Ministerial Effectiveness Seminars were designed to help clergy break out of maintenance mode ministry and utilize the insights of the new "science" of church growth.

Growth Plus is a creation of Joe Harding's to train ordained clergy as professional consultants who spend three days observing, listening, and guiding a local church. Forty pastors were certified as Consultants.

Congregational Development must involve the organization of new churches. An $8 million capital campaign for land purchase, bricks and mortar, and congregational remissioning is being used to "jump start" a re-entry into unchurched areas and the development of parish ministry for those so often overlooked by today's mainline churches— the poor, the ethnic minority, and those who have lost their way in life, succumbing to either substance addiction or behavioral addiction which they cannot escape save by the redeeming grace of a loving God.

Mobilization of a judicatory is a massive challenge, but Vision 2000 has become a "household" word. The principles and practices taught to local church laity and clergy resulted in a resounding reversal of a downward membership trend. In 1990 the WNC Conference of The United Methodist Church had a net gain of 1624 members, 5155 constituents (prospective members), 3946 in average Sunday morning attendance, and 802 more children in Sunday school every Sunday!

Donald W. Haynes,
Director of Ministries
Western North Carolina Conference

ENDNOTES

[1] John Naisbitt and Patricia Aburdene, *Megatrends 2000* (New York: William Morrow, 1988), p. 11.

[2] Bill Lawren, *Psychology Today.* Reprinted with permission from *Psychology Today Magazine*, Copyright © 1989 (PT Partners, L.P.).

[3] Barna research group, *America 2000: What the Trends Mean for Christianity* (Barna Research Group, P.O. Box 4152, Glendale, CA 91222-0152), p. 35.

[4] Naisbitt and Aburdene, p. 11.

[5] Rackman Holt, *Mary McLeod Bethune* (New York: Doubleday and Co. Inc., Copyright 1964), p. 45. Used by permission of Doubleday & Co., Inc.

[6] Teo Furtado, *Pursuits Magazine* (Fall, 1989), p. 22. Reprinted with permission from *Pursuits*. Copyright © 1989, Whittle Communications L.P.

[7] Ibid.

[8] Donald Wilson, *My Six Convicts* (Rinehart, 1951).

[9] Tom Peters, *Thriving on Chaos: Handbook for a Management Revolution* (New York: Alfred A. Knopf Inc. Publishers, 1987), pp. 260, 261. Used by permission of Alfred A. Knopf Inc.

[10] Ibid.

[11] World Future Society, 4916 Saint Elmo Ave., Bethesda, MD 20814. Used by permission.

[12] Russell Chandler, *Understanding the New Age* (Dallas: Word Incorporated Publishers, 1988), p. 22. Used by permission.

[13] Ibid.

[14] George Gallup, Jr. and Jim Castelli, *The People's Religion* (New York: Macmillan Publishing Company, 1989), pp. 56, 58, 68, 37. Reprinted with permission of Macmillan Publishing Company.

[15] Earl G. Hunt, Jr., *I Have Believed: A Bishop Talks About His Faith* (Nashville, TN: The Upper Room, 1980). Used by permission of the publisher.

[16] Lyle Schaller, *The Multiple Staff and the Larger Church* (Nashville, TN: Abingdon, 1980).

[17] Richard Erdoes, *A.D. 1000: Living on the Brink of the Apocalypse* (New York: Harper and Row, 1988).

SUGGESTED RESOURCES

The following books are available from Discipleship Resources, toll-free (800) 685-4370 or fax (404) 442-5114, unless indicated otherwise:

Baby Boomer Spirituality. Craig K. Miller. DR106.

Beyond the Walls: A Congregational Guide for Lifestyle Relational Evangelism. James W. Hollis, Jr. DR124.

Building God's People. Thomas R. Hawkins. LA070.

Christian Education Planning Handbook. Roy Ryan. 0860C.

The Church Finance Idea Book. Wayne C. Barrett. DR065.

Come and See: Biblical and Contemporary Encounters with Christ. Shirley F. Clement. EV182.

Covenant Discipleship: Christian Formation Through Mutual Accountability. David Lowes Watson. DR091.

Encounters with Jesus. Craig K. Miller. DR113.

Evangelism Ministries Planning Handbook. Suzanne G. Braden. EV154.

Every Member in Ministry. John Ed Mathison. EV162.

Extending Your Congregation's Welcome. W. James Cowell. DR068.

Faith-Sharing: Dynamic Christian Witnessing by Invitation. George E. Morris and H. Eddie Fox. DR039.

Gifts Discovery Workshop. Herbert Mather. ST046 and ST045.

Grace-Esteem: New Life in Christ. H. Eddie Fox. DR069.

Growing New Churches. Stephen C. Compton and G. Steven Sallee. DR115.

Growth Plus: The Vision. Joe A. Harding. DR052.

Incorporating New Members. W. James Cowell. DR112.

In the Meantime: A Study on the Kingdom of God. H. Eddie Fox and Shirley F. Clement. EV181.

Lay Witness Mission Handbook. Shirley F. Clement. EV183.

More Money, New Money, Big Money. Wayne C. Barrett. DR120.

Putting God First: The Tithe. Norma Wimberly. DR058.

Small Groups: Getting Started. Suzanne G. Braden and Shirley F. Clement. EV175.

Tried and True. John Ed Mathison. DR117.

Vision 2000: Worship Attendance Crusade Guide. Joe A. Harding. EV184.

THE FOLLOWING BOOKS ARE AVAILABLE FROM ABINGDON PRESS:

Church Growth Handbook. Bill Easum. 081610.

Church Growth: Strategies That Work. Donald McGavran and George G. Hunter III. 081602.

44 Ways to Expand the Financial Base of Your Congregation. Lyle Schaller. 13286X.

44 Ways to Increase Church Attendance. Lyle Schaller. 132878.

How to Build a Magnetic Church. Herb Miller. 177626.

How to Reach Secular People. George G. Hunter III. 179300.

Let the Redeemed of the Lord Say So. H. Eddie Fox and George Morris. 213800.

The Small Church Is Different! Lyle Schaller. 387175.

The Vital Congregation. Herb Miller. 437962.

OTHER RESOURCES:

America 2000: What the Trends Mean for Christianity. A Barna Report—Ministry Information from the Barna Research Group, P. O. Box 4152, Glendale, CA 91222-0152.

American Demographics Magazine. A publication of Dow Jones and Company Inc.

The Futurist Magazine. A journal of forecasts, trends, and ideas about the future.

Megatrends 2000. John Naisbitt and Patricia Aburdene. William Morrow and Company, Inc. New York.

What Lies Ahead: Countdown to the 21st Century. United Way Strategic Institute. 701 North Fairfax Street, Alexandria, VA 22314-2045.